The Mindful Twenty-Something

Life Skills To Handle Stress ... & Everything Else

Holly B. Rogers, MD

16

EasyRead Large

Read How You Want

LARGE PRINT BOOKS, BRAILLE & DAISY

Copyright Page from the Original Book

Library of Congress Cataloging-in-Publication Data on file

TABLE OF CONTENTS

"Given the current state of higher education today, to call *The Mindful Twenty-Something* timely is an understatement. The conversational tone offers an approachable presentation of mindfulness appropriate for many of the complexities that modern undergraduate and graduate students face. The simple practices outlined in this book ensure both the accessibility and applicability of mindfulness and will undoubtedly be a valuable resource not only for students but those working with contemplation in higher education."
—**Jason Jones, PhD,** Contemplative Sciences Center, University of Virginia

"Based in ancient contemplative wisdom, modern science, and Holly Rogers' extensive experience working with college students and young adults, this book is an excellent resource for a person of 'any-something' age who wishes to begin or learn more about practicing mindfulness."
—**Jeff Brantley, MD,** assistant consulting professor in the department of psychiatry and behavioral sciences at Duke University Medical Center; founding faculty member of Duke Integrative Medicine, and founder and director of its Mindfulness Based Stress Reduction (MBSR) program; and author of *Calming Your Angry Mind*

"Mystified by meditation? Engaging, accessible, and down to earth, *The Mindful Twenty-Something* has everything you need to start meditating and more."
—Sumi Loundon Kim, Buddhist chaplain at Duke University

"Easy to read and immensely practical, *The Mindful Twenty-Something* is a 21st century book, grounded in ancient ways of practice. In it, Holly Rogers' professional experience and her love of mindful practice come together in a way that will be of great benefit to many."
—Sharon Salzberg, author of *Lovingkindness* and *Real Happiness*

"In *The Mindful Twenty-Something,* Holly invites young people to explore mindfulness and meditation with a curious and open mind. With warmth and a clear, direct tone, she speaks candidly about the precious and fleeting nature of our lives, advocating that mindfulness and meditation are the path to fully engaging with the present moment. Allowing for skepticism and doubt, this book helps bridge the gap between understanding mindfulness and developing a regular meditation practice."
—Jeanne Mahon, MEd, director of the Center for Wellness at Harvard University

"Having just shepherded two daughters through their twenties, I can say with confidence that it is not an easy time these days, and the statistics on mental health challenges for that age group bear that out. Holly Rogers not only knows plenty of people trying to start out their lives during that difficult stage, but she cares deeply about what they need. In this book, she offers insights and practical tools that will shape the present and the future of many young people."

—Barry Boyce, editor in chief at *Mindful* magazine and mindful.org

"Holly Rogers has written a unique introduction to becoming mindful, deeply grounded in her own experience. She has both practiced herself for years and taught students at Duke, and the book reflects both. Wise, but not obscure. Practical, but lighthearted and inspiring."

—Mirabai Bush, meditation and mindfulness teacher, cofounder and senior fellow of the Center for Contemplative Mind in Society, and coauthor of *Contemplative Practices in Higher Education*

For Bill, Nick, Will, and Maggie Rose

Each one of us is a visitor to this planet, a guest who has only a finite time to stay. What greater folly could there be than to spend this short time lonely, unhappy, and in conflict with our fellow visitors? Far better, surely, to use our short time in pursuing a meaningful life, enriched by a sense of connection with and service toward others.

—Dalai Lama

Introduction

Let's start with my story, and then I'll take a shot at yours. When I was just past my thirtieth birthday, I moved to New Zealand by myself to take my first real job as a psychiatrist. It was a big step for me, leaving the security of my training program, family, and friends. It turned out to be a great decision, and the year I worked there is easily one of the most memorable of my life.

When it came time to return to the States, I was filled with considerable uncertainty. I missed all my people at home, but I also loved my life in New Zealand. As I made my way back to North Carolina, I was dealing with a hefty load of worry and self-doubt.

On my long journey home, I came across a book called *Mindfulness in Plain English* (Gunaratana 1996). I picked it up because I was curious about the meaning of the title. I'd never heard of mindfulness, and frankly, it seemed to already be in plain English.

As I thumbed through the book, I was quickly captured by what I found. The author explained that there was this thing called *mindfulness,* an approach to life that involved learning to give the bulk of your attention to your present-moment experience, instead of wasting time worrying about the future or regretting the past. This approach would allow me to experience greater satisfaction and peace of mind, and it was something that anyone could learn by practicing a particular technique called *mindfulness meditation.*

I was intrigued and decided to give it a try. First chance I had, I piled some pillows on the floor and plopped down to begin meditating. Following the instructions in the book, I was hoping for instant peace of mind. You can imagine my disappointment to discover instead discomfort.

For me, it was at first painfully hard to sit still and witness my rapidly turning mind. Until that moment, I had no idea that the contents of my mind were such a crazy, hurly-burly mess through which I filtered my entire life experience. I didn't know that sitting still for a few minutes was beyond me. I didn't like the idea that I couldn't do it; the challenge of it drew me in.

When I got back to North Carolina, I found a teacher, joined a meditation group, and started attending meditation retreats. Though at first it was hard work, before long I began to experience a number of the profound changes that a mindfulness practice promised. I worried less about the future, found more joy in life's simple pleasures, and became more clear about what I wanted from life. As time went by, I frequently found myself thinking, *I wish someone had taught me this when I was in medical school,* because I knew my educational experience would have been enhanced by mindfulness practice during those years.

Okay. Now it's time for your story.

Your Emerging Adult Story

If you are somewhere been eighteen and twenty-nine years old, you are in the life stage known as *emerging adulthood,* and this book is written for you. Because the term *emerging adult* is a little stiff or formal, I will mostly refer to my readers as young adults or twenty-somethings, though I am including folks in their late teens as well.

Of course everybody is different, but if you are in your late teens or twenties, you probably have a number of traits in common with your age-mates, regardless of your race, religion, gender, sexual orientation, or socioeconomic status (Arnett 2004).

If you are like most people, young adulthood is the first stage of life in which you get to make all your own decisions. Everything from what time you go to bed to how much money you will spend is entirely up to you. Typically during this time you put a lot of energy into exploring the two big spheres of life: your career goals and your love life.

Most people in their twenties don't yet have all the responsibilities, financial or personal, that will structure life down the road, leaving them remarkably free to explore. It's an exciting time of life filled with change; you may be frequently switching jobs, majors, roommates, or lovers. It's of course fun, but it also gets scary sometimes. Constant change and uncertainty can be hard to manage. Struggling to pay the rent or repay student loans, working while going to school, dealing with a bad breakup—these typical stressors for young adults can become overwhelming at times.

Wonderfully, twenty-somethings are curious, energetic, and open-minded. Typically, people your age are willing to learn new things and take on new challenges, and most of you are optimistic that you will get what you want out of life (Arnett 2004).

So even though I don't know your particular story, I can guess that you are facing lots of challenges, often having a great deal of fun, sometimes feeling overwhelmed, and mostly feeling hopeful about what the future will bring. And, what's more, you really want your life to be meaningful.

Mindfulness in Your Twenties

Because of the changes and challenges you encounter in your late teens and twenties, it's a great time to learn to live mindfully. Mindfulness develops self-awareness that informs all of your important life choices. It helps you manage your stress and maintain peace of mind. It helps you connect with all the marvelous moments in your day so that you don't miss out on any of the fun of your wild ride through life.

Getting back to my story, remember how I wish I'd learned mindfulness even earlier in life? Now let's fast forward a couple years to the time that I took a job as one of the psychiatrists in the student counseling center at Duke University, in Durham, North Carolina.

Because of my own experience with mindfulness, I was excited by the possibility of sharing mindfulness with all the young adults I found myself surrounded by. Though this seemed like a decent idea, I soon learned that it was harder than I expected. The Duke students were very busy and didn't have a lot of time to devote to learning something new. Additionally, many were skeptical about whether it would be worth their while to learn this seemingly strange activity.

To make a very long story short, it took me years to find a way to make mindfulness useful and compelling to the students. Luckily, I met Margaret Maytan, a psychiatrist in training at Duke who was also interested in teaching mindfulness. With lots of trial and error, and lots of great feedback from our students, over the course of several years Margaret and I crafted a program that proved both popular and effective (Greeson et al. 2014). We named it *Koru,* the New Zealand Māori word for the spiral shape of the new fern frond, a shape that symbolizes new, balanced growth. The Māori people have a reverence for nature and a balanced approach to life that reflects many of the values of mindfulness. Koru is now taught all over the US and abroad and, at the time of this writing, is the only evidence-based mindfulness program designed particularly for young adults.

I've been so amazed by the transformation I've seen in our Koru students that I got the itch to try to reach even more young adults who might benefit from mindfulness. Besides, Koru needed a text for its students. Thus, this book that you are reading.

Author's Note

I keep notebooks that I fill with stories from the students I teach mindfulness to, both in my Koru classes and in other settings. The stories in this book are drawn from those notebooks. The names and details have been changed to make the students unrecognizable to my readers and, perhaps, even to themselves.

How to Use This Book

This book is designed to nudge you into trying mindfulness. In my experience, bridging the gap between understanding that mindfulness is a helpful skill and actually practicing it in a meaningful way is the trickiest part. *The Mindful Twenty-Something* is about helping you across that gap, taking you from a solid understanding of mindfulness and its benefits to a regular practice that produces positive changes for you.

I've already begun to hint at some of the benefits of mindfulness. I suppose it wouldn't be surprising if these claims trigger a mix of curiosity and skepticism in you. Fortunately, that mix is the perfect place to start on any worthwhile exploration.

There's only one way to find out whether mindfulness will be useful for you personally; you'll have to try it and see. I'm hoping you will find this book a helpful guide for that process.

If you are up for it, I'd suggest you conduct your personal experiment in mindfulness this way:

- Read a few pages of this book every day. When you see a passage marked "Contemplate This" or "Take a Moment," spend a few moments to reflect on the passage or do the suggested exercise.

- Spend ten minutes each day practicing one of the skills or meditations I'll be introducing throughout the book. *If you do nothing else, do this.* It's the only way to see whether this stuff works for you.
- Keep a log of your daily practice. Write down some thoughts about the experience each day.
- Every day, record two things that are positive in your life or that you could be grateful for. (Skip to chapter 10 if you are curious about why this is helpful.)
- Don't expect yourself to be perfect. If you miss a day, don't give up; just pick up where you left off the next day and keep going.
- Try being mindful as you go about your day. Pick an activity you typically do mindlessly every day, like brushing your teeth or putting on your socks. Each time you do that activity, pay very close attention to every sensation, thought, and feeling associated with it. Each week, pick a different activity. To help you remember, write down (somewhere you will see it) the activity you plan to do mindfully.
- Hold off on assessing the benefits of mindfulness for yourself until you have made it all the way to the end of the book.

Sounds like a lot to keep organized, doesn't it? If you are thinking there must be an app for that, you are right! If you want, you can download the Koru Mindfulness app to your smartphone or tablet and use the guided meditations and video demonstrations to help you with your practice. With the app you can also log your meditations, track your weekly mindfulness activity, make entries on the gratitude wall, and connect with others who are learning to meditate.

Don't have the app? No worries. It is totally unnecessary for your experiment. Instead, put a small notebook in an eye-catching spot and record your meditations, reflections, and gratitudes there. For some extra help, you can find all the Koru Mindfulness meditations and skills at http://www.korumindfulness.org/guided -meditations.

Time to Get Started

So here's the deal. You can read this book without doing any of the stuff listed above. It will teach you a lot about mindfulness and how it can potentially be useful for you. But you won't actually experience any change unless you put some time into practicing. Like learning any other skill, from shooting baskets to playing the piano, mindfulness takes practice.

Remember, you have this book in your hand for a reason. Either you were curious enough to pick it up yourself, or someone you know thought you needed it. If you want to satisfy your curiosity about whether mindfulness will work for you, this is your chance to find out. Just dig in and do it. Now is a great time to get started.

Part 1

Getting Ready

Chapter 1

This Is Your Life. Don't Miss It.

What are you waiting for? To get past the next test or finish the semester? To graduate? To find the right job or make more money? To lose ten pounds or bench press 200 pounds? To find the perfect life partner?

Our lives are a freaking miracle, but if we don't wake up and pay attention, we are liable to miss much of the thrill of our time-limited ride on this beautiful planet. If you frequently have thoughts that begin, *As soon as this is over I will start...,* then you are in the habit of pushing your full engagement in life off into some foggy, distant future.

You are in good company; almost everybody does this to some degree. Young adults are particularly prone to this. Because your focus in your late teens and twenties is on constructing the foundation for the rest of your life, it's natural to dwell on what that life will look like.

Even though much of the activity of your current life seems to be in preparation for your future life, the only life you actually have is the one happening right this very second. As one of the students in my mindfulness class said, "I realized that if I am not really living in the present now, what makes me think I'll start doing it in the future?" Excellent question. Maybe now is the best time to change this habit.

Many people go through life as if they can only relax and enjoy things once all the external factors (jobs, relationships, finances) are just the way they want them. If this is your perspective, I invite you to challenge that belief. For one thing, the future that you are waiting for will never arrive. There will always be one more thing to complete or accomplish before you get "there."

For another thing, the external factors of your life don't determine your happiness as much as you think they do. We all believe if we had the best body or the hottest lover, made the most money or had the highest GRE score, then we'd be happy. But for how long? Not very long, as it turns out.

Our victories don't generally keep us satisfied for long because it's not the circumstances of our lives that primarily determine our happiness. In fact, the actual circumstances of our lives have relatively little to do with our general level of happiness (Lyubomirsky, Sheldon, and Schkade 2005). Instead, it is largely the way we think about and relate to the events of our lives that influences whether we live with great satisfaction or intense suffering. Getting clear on this particular misconception has the potential to significantly improve your life.

You probably know someone (or are someone?) who seems to have everything he could possibly want, but still feels miserable, dissatisfied, and worried about his lot in life. We hear stories of millionaires who commit suicide, feeling great despair despite truly having every comfort available on this planet. Conversely, we've all heard stories of individuals who have suffered horrific experiences and yet live with great contentment.

The other day, I heard a story about a man now living in the United States, a refugee from a war-torn country and the only survivor of his family, who earns his income shining shoes and thus lives in relative poverty. This man takes great pride in his work and treats all his customers with sincere kindness. His story was drawing attention because people were so moved by his ability to live with such happiness and integrity despite the extremely difficult circumstances of his life.

Of course, it's important to recognize that there are life circumstances that are seriously problematic; my intent is not to trivialize the magnitude of suffering caused by abuse, prejudice, oppression, and poverty. Obviously, it would be absurd to tell those who are living with these injustices that they just need to change their attitude rather than acknowledge that real-world solutions are needed for these problems. At the same time, almost all forms of suffering can be diminished, even if ever so slightly, by internal shifts in our approach to our difficulties. Mindfulness allows you to make those internal shifts.

Mindfulness Is a Game Changer

Mindfulness is the act of paying attention to your present-moment experience with an attitude of compassionate curiosity. Rather than worrying about the future or rehashing the past, you hold your attention on the moment at hand.

The ability to be mindful is actually a capacity that is naturally present in all of us, though most of us haven't spent much time developing it. Mindfulness has been around as an approach for managing suffering since at least 2,500 years ago, when the Buddha discovered the power of mindfulness on his journey to enlightenment, but it has only recently become a well-known and widely accepted concept in the West.

Mindfulness helps you develop the internal conditions that lead to enduring happiness so that you are not so vulnerable to the constantly changing external conditions of your life experience. Thus, it offers you the opportunity to maintain your peace of mind no matter what events you encounter.

CONTEMPLATE THIS:

Peace. It does not mean to be in a place where there is no noise, trouble or hard work. It means to be in the midst of those things and still be calm in your heart.

—Unknown

Say Good-Bye to the Mind-Body Divide

There is a great deal of solid, scientific evidence that learning to focus your attention without judgment on the present has a positive impact on much of your life, from improving your ability to focus efficiently on your work to helping you manage your emotions in difficult situations. Further, it increases your capacity to experience positive emotions such as contentment, compassion, awe, and gratitude.

A short list of medical conditions that have been shown to improve with mindfulness includes eating disorders, attention-deficit/hyper-activity disorder (ADHD), chronic pain, depression, high blood pressure, cardiac illness, anxiety, and substance abuse and addiction. Almost all stress-related conditions will improve with regular mindfulness training. Additionally, mindfulness improves test scores, sleep, and memory. It boosts immune function and reduces stress hormones.

At first glance, it may seem a bit surprising that just by changing the way you focus your attention you can impact the physical workings of your body, including your brain and nervous system. But in fact, there is no separation between body and mind. Body is mind; mind is body. It's all molecules joining, separating, moving together in the great dance of life. Every thought *(I think I'll watch one more show before I start on my project)* or emotion (irritation at being stuck behind a slow-moving car) you experience is caused by chemicals moving between the nerve cells in your brain, producing physical changes that are experienced as thoughts and emotions.

Shifting your thoughts by controlling the direction of your attention both causes and is caused by the firing of the nerve cells that make up your brain, producing a wide range of responses in your nervous system and beyond. Thus, simply paying attention to how you pay attention can affect outcomes such as the robustness of your immune response and the size of certain regions of your brain.

Science Note: If you are doubtful that altering your thoughts can have any tangible, physical consequences, then you might be surprised to learn that men can increase their beard growth just by changing what they think about!

Way back in the twentieth century—1970 to be exact—a scientist anonymously published a study in the journal *Nature* proving that just thinking about sex made a man's beard grow faster. He was clearly a scientist with time on his hands and sex on his mind. At the time, he was living in isolation on an island during the week, and on the weekends he would return to the mainland to hook up with "particular female company." He observed that his beard would grow more rapidly on Fridays as he began to anticipate his weekend of sexual pleasure.

The scientist had an obsessive streak, I guess, because he started weighing his shavings each day and graphing the results. The findings were striking, showing a clear increase in beard growth on the day before and days during sexual activity. Most surprisingly, his beard growth was highest the day *before* he had sex, when he was just *thinking* an awful lot about having sex.

Presumably, the increased beard growth was due to increases in testosterone. Testosterone increases when men are sexually active, and beards grow faster when there is a lot of testosterone in the mix ("Effects of Sexual Activity on Beard Growth in Man" 1970).

This is a perfect demonstration of how the content of our thoughts can produce measurable, physical changes.

Some Important Points About Mindfulness

Listed below are a few points about mindfulness that I think may be particularly pertinent for you and that I will revisit throughout this book. Mindfulness is both straightforward and complicated. Some aspects of it bear repeating. Don't worry too much about understanding the significance of everything on this list right now. I just want to give you a sense of the ground we will cover as we learn the practice of mindfulness and explore the broad consequences of developing a mindful approach to life.

1. *A new perspective.* The practice of mindfulness essentially involves learning a different way of attending to the events

and experiences of your life, both internal ones (thoughts, emotions, sensations) and external ones (other people, your wins, your losses, the weather).

2. *It takes practice.* Mindfulness is in part a practice because it takes practice. The more you work at it, the greater the impact it will have in your life. There are a number of ways to practice mindfulness, all of which involve some time spent in silence, developing the skill of focusing your attention on your present-moment experience. This resting in silence is typically referred to as meditating. You, of course, can call it whatever you like.

3. *Nonjudgment.* A critical part of mindfulness practice is learning to observe what is happening without automatically judging or categorizing it as good or bad, right or wrong. Once you become skilled at removing the filter of judgment from your observations, you will have a more accurate and clear picture of your life experience.

4. *Observing mind.* Learning to see things this way requires the development of your observing mind, the part of your mind that watches thoughts and reactions but is not involved so much in creating them.

5. *Insights.* Through the practice of mindfulness, you develop important insights into the way life works. You develop

awareness of what you value and what is meaningful. These insights will guide you as you make choices about all aspects of your life, from whom you spend your time with to how you approach your work.

Mindfulness Is Not...

Here are a couple things that mindfulness is not.

Mindfulness Is Not a Religion

Mindfulness and meditation may be integrated into spiritual and religious practices, but they are not a religion per se. Though mindfulness is rooted historically and philosophically in Buddhism, mindfulness meditation reflects only a very small sliver of all that is encompassed by Buddhism. Buddhism is an ancient and complex religion and philosophy that has a vast multitude of beliefs, rituals, and practices associated with it in its various forms. In short, the learning of mindfulness meditation is neither necessary nor sufficient for participating in Buddhism as a religion. Conversely, practicing the religion of Buddhism is not at all necessary to incorporate mindfulness into your life.

Sometimes people new to mindfulness wonder whether it will conflict with their personal spiritual practices and belief systems. In my experience, this does not tend to be the case. As a matter of fact, most faith traditions have some form of meditation or prayer that has features in common with mindfulness meditation. Many people find that practicing mindfulness enhances their connection to their personal faith. Over the last twenty or so years of teaching mindfulness to students at Duke University, I have had the privilege of listening to students from almost every faith tradition talk about their personal journeys integrating mindfulness into their spiritual practice.

CONTEMPLATE THIS:

We must allow each other our differences at the same time as we recognize our sameness.

—Audre Lorde

Mindfulness Is Not a Panacea for All Ills

Let's be honest. There is a lot of hype these days praising the benefits of mindfulness. It can be a bit obnoxious at times and may leave an exaggerated impression that mindfulness will solve whatever problems you have and end all suffering in your life. Oh, how I wish that were true. But it's not. Because you are human, no matter how diligent your mindfulness practice is, you will still have problems, including the big three unavoidable ones that started the Buddha on his spiritual quest: old age, sickness, and death. You will also have other problems: bad grades, missed flights, dead-end jobs, car trouble, money trouble, fights with your lovers, and so on.

Mindfulness will not eliminate all difficulties from your life, but it can diminish how disruptive they are. Mindfulness teaches you a different approach to the inevitable ups and downs of life, an approach that improves your resilience so that you stay on your feet and keep moving. It's pretty hard to actually understand how this all works until you have some experience with mindfulness, so for now, see whether you can just stay open to the possibility that this is true and develop the willingness to try it out and see what happens.

Making a Choice

So what's it going to be? Who are you going to be? Someone who lives your life always thinking about what you don't have, waiting until the weekend or next year to see what is right in front of you? Or are you going to be someone who is open to the magic in every moment, including the good, the bad, and everything in between? If you want to show up and be present for your life, then read on. You can learn how.

Chapter 2

"Do I Really Have to Meditate?"

Do you really have to meditate? Yes, and this is why. Living mindfully is an attitude and a particular approach to life, but it is also in part a skill, like juggling or playing the kazoo. It is not an innate talent. Anyone can do it, but it takes practice, and meditation is the way you practice mindfulness.

In the modern world, we live in an anti-mindfulness culture that values multitasking and rapid shifting of focus. When you first try to focus on one thing at a time with patience and curiosity, it will probably not come easily. You may notice some version of the thought *This just isn't for me* or *This is a stinking waste of time,* which if taken too literally could end any progress toward greater mindfulness.

With practice, though, you learn to notice these and other thoughts without getting caught up in them. You begin to see that they are simply words or images produced by your mind that reflect your restlessness in the moment. They don't speak "truth" about the value of meditation or your ability to do it.

Meditation Is Exercise for Your Brain

Though training your brain is as important as training your body, most people don't recognize this. Just as you get faster by running three miles a day or get stronger by lifting weights, you can become more mindful by practicing meditation. Often we refer to meditation practice as "building your mindfulness muscle." Most young adults are willing to devote hours a week to working toward fitter, more attractive bodies. Might it be worth putting in some time to develop a fitter mind as well?

Think about it. If I told you that I would give you a million dollars if you could bench press 200 pounds, what would your reaction be? Would you think, *Darn, too bad I'm not that strong?* More likely you would start working out straight away, knowing you had a lot of weight lifting in front of you to get that chunk of change. Of course you wouldn't begin by trying to lift 200 pounds; you'd start with 20 pounds or 50 pounds and slowly work your way up to the heavier weight.

It's exactly the same with mindfulness training. The lightest weight of mindfulness training is a few minutes of meditation, seated in a comfortable chair in a quiet location. Slightly heavier weights are longer durations of time or less ideal conditions.

We lift these lighter weights so that we are ready for the heavy lifting that life will inevitably provide. Everyone's heavy weight will be different, but situations such as performing poorly on an important exam, dealing with a difficult boss, or fighting with friends and family members can feel like 200-pound emotional weights. These are also the situations that will become less stressful and easier to "lift" as your mindfulness skills progress.

Science Note: Fortunately, it doesn't take that much meditation practice to start to experience the benefits of mindfulness. In our study of Koru, the meditation program we developed for students at Duke University, we found that ten minutes a day of mindfulness practice for four weeks had a significant impact on our students' lives, helping them sleep better, feel less stressed, be more mindful, and have greater self-compassion (Greeson et al. 2014). So only a few minutes a day for a few weeks can produce meaningful change. That seems doable, doesn't it?

Meditation Is No Big Deal

The good news is that meditating is truly not that big a deal. The word evokes a surprisingly wide range of responses in different people, some of which may arise from misconceptions about what meditation actually involves. Whether you think it sounds boring or fascinating, exotic or mundane, you can be curious and give it a try.

Breath Awareness Meditation

Wherever you are right now, read through this meditation, and then do it.

Close your eyes. Pay attention to your breathing and see whether you can find the place in your body where you most clearly feel the sensations of your breath moving in and out. You might notice it at the tip of your nose or in the rise and fall of your belly or chest. It makes no difference at all where you feel your breath; there's no "right" place.

Got it? Okay, now just let your attention settle on that place, and watch your breath as it moves in and back out. With an attitude of relaxed curiosity, count ten breaths. Don't try to change or control your breathing. You don't need to do any special or fancy breathing. Just count ten inhalations and ten exhalations.

You may notice that your mind wanders quickly, maybe even before the end of the first breath. When that happens, without judging yourself or your wandering mind, bring your attention back to your breath. Stop after you've completed ten breaths.

So, what do you think? You have just completed about a minute of meditation. Was that unpleasant or particularly strange? Do that nine more times and you will have completed the amount of meditation practice that I am going to encourage you to do each day.

The meditation you just practiced is a breath awareness meditation, a commonly practiced type of meditation. Because the breath is always present and always changing, it makes an ideal focus for your attention. Breath awareness is by no means the only type of meditation, but it is the most common one and an easy one to get started with. You'll have the chance to learn other types as you make your way through this book.

Practice Tip: Finding the right posture is important when you are meditating; it is hard to stay alert when slouching. If you are using a chair, pick one with a straight back, not a recliner. If you are sitting on a cushion on the floor, make sure your seat is elevated a few inches off the floor so that when you sit cross-legged, your pelvis tilts forward and down, which is the most stable and comfortable position.

Either on cushions on the floor or seated in a chair, sit with your back tall, the crown of your head extending toward the sky. Let your hands rest comfortably in your lap.

Keep your ears in line above your shoulders, tuck your chin, and relax your shoulders. Though sitting tall, you don't want to be stiff or uncomfortable, feeling constantly tempted to wiggle. A wiggling body will inevitably produce a wiggling mind—not what you are aiming for.

What Is the Goal Supposed to Be?

Jackie said to me in her second Koru class, "What is my goal supposed to be when I'm meditating?" Jackie, a typical hard-driving student, was voicing one of the most frequent questions I hear. You need to know what you are trying to accomplish when you sit down to meditate, right?

There are two levels of goals to consider when you are developing a mindfulness practice. First is the larger life goal that might drive your motivation to develop a meditation practice in the first place. These types of goals are usually something like wanting to manage stress more effectively or to find a better way to deal with some physical or emotional challenge.

The second goal is the more immediate goal you have when you sit down to meditate. What are you trying to achieve while you are actually in the process of meditating? This in-the-moment goal is the one I am most commonly asked about, so I'm going to do my best to give you a straight answer.

Your goal during a meditation practice is very simply to *fully inhabit* the present moment by holding your awareness on the sensation of your breath or some other sensory experience. Inhabiting the present moment establishes the conditions that *may* produce a stable state of concentration in which you are aware of your thoughts and feelings without engaging with them or reacting to them. If you achieve this level of awareness, you will experience an interesting state that is hard to describe but tends to be very satisfying, even blissful. It feels spacious, with room for whatever arises to move about. Though your reactivity is much lower, you still feel intensely. There is not a numb quality to it. In fact everything seems quite vivid. Often there is a profound sense of well-being. A strong sense of connection to others emerges, and feelings of compassion naturally arise.

To be honest, you are unlikely to experience this fully in just ten minutes of meditation. This type of concentrative state typically takes longer to develop, and it takes quite a bit of practice. As your mindfulness muscle builds, you will likely start to get glimpses of it. If you are willing to spend more time practicing, your ability to inhabit this conscious space will expand, though it is definitely not something that can be forced.

Now, please forget all about this blissful state or you will never achieve it. You cannot force this level of consciousness to open up for you by striving hard in pursuit of it. As a matter of fact, I might get kicked out of the Meditation Teachers Guild for even acknowledging that you might try to set a goal of achieving a blissful mind state. Why? Because accepting each moment as it is—non-striving—is an absolutely essential element of mindfulness meditation.

Non-striving is the bedrock of mindfulness. It may seem irrational, but it is a fundamental truth of this practice that you can only achieve these states by being completely unattached to achieving them. All you can do is create the conditions that allow for these mind states to develop, and you do that by simply and fully inhabiting the present moment. You have to be completely willing for things to be exactly as they are before they start to become something different. And you can't cheat; there's no getting around this.

So, what is the goal when you sit down to practice? The goal is to have no goals other than being fully present and curious about each and every moment.

Working with the Rushing River of Thought

There's one more thing you need to know about meditating to avoid complete frustration: meditation is not about stopping your thoughts. I would be so rich if I had a nickel for every time a student has said to me, "I can't get my thoughts to stop." If you try to stop your thoughts, you will fail, and then you will hate it and then you will quit. So don't do it.

Our brains make thoughts. That is what the human brain is built to do, and it will keep doing that until the moment of your death. With meditation you are not trying to stop those thoughts; you are just trying to change your relationship to them.

Your mind is a rushing river of thoughts. The river never stops, but it is constantly changing. Sometimes it is wild with crashing waves. Sometimes it is flowing more quietly. When you meditate, you are not trying to stop the river and dam the thoughts (or damn the thoughts, for that matter!). You are just trying to get out of the stream so you don't drown.

When you meditate, you climb onto the bank and watch the river. Most people fall right back in the river before they get to the end of the next breath, so you will find that what you are really practicing is catching yourself when you fall back in and then climbing back out.

You'll quickly see that sitting on the bank observing the river with curiosity and patience feels very different from being in the river, caught up in the current.

If you keep practicing, you will become familiar with the contents of your personal river. You'll see funny eddies that drag certain thoughts around and around. You'll see little waves that you had no idea existed in your river. You'll probably find that at times the river slows a bit and you can sit on the bank more comfortably. Over time, you might start to find it all a bit humorous. So when you see *I can't stop my thoughts* floating by, just stay on the bank and let it move on down the river.

Start Your Meditation Practice Now

If you truly want to develop the ability to live mindfully, you will need to meditate regularly. For now, I invite you to do the breath awareness meditation described above. Set the timer on your phone or other device, and practice focusing your attention on your breath sensations for just ten minutes. You may see that what you are really practicing is your willingness to gather up your attention and bring it back to one point, over and over. Though it is simple, it is not easy, which is why it takes practice. Right now could be the best time to start practicing.

Part 2

Getting Started

Chapter 3

Mindfulness for Calming and Focusing

In this chapter, I'll introduce the first set of mindfulness skills for you to begin practicing as you make your way through this book. If you have made it this far into a book on mindfulness, there is some reason for your interest. It is possible that I am such a compelling author that my writing is irresistible, but I doubt it. If you are like the majority of people who come to Koru and want to learn mindfulness, you are probably motivated in part by feeling worn down by all the stress in your life.

In my experience, trouble caused by stress can manifest in any number of ways. Here are some examples. Amir felt tense and had a hard time sleeping. He often felt tired and his body ached because he could not shut off his mind and fall asleep at night. Yan was plagued with frequent worry; her mind never stopped planning, as she imagined every possible contingency and how she could either prevent or deal with each scenario she created. Dan noted that he often felt disconnected and bored, like he was on a hamster wheel, spinning fast and going nowhere; he said he only had "fun" if he was drunk or high. Keandra said that she felt irritable and snapped impatiently at her friends when stressed.

TAKE A MOMENT: How do you typically manifest stress? Do you do any of the things described above, or is your stress response different? Pay attention to the way your body signals that your stress level has gotten too high. Awareness of your personal stress red flags will alert you to intentionally de-stress before you become overwhelmed.

Breath and Body Sensation Awareness

Given that feeling stressed, overwhelmed, or dissatisfied is often what motivates people to take up mindfulness, it's best to start with skills that directly address these challenges. The skills in this chapter are all about helping you calm down and learn to focus your attention.

Below you will find instructions for three awareness exercises that will build your mindfulness muscle and help you manage your feelings of stress. Over the next few days, try them each several times and see what you think. My hope is that you will try all the skills and meditations in this book, and by the time you get to the end you will have found a handful that are particularly useful to you and that you practice regularly.

Belly Breathing to Calm Your Body and Mind

The diaphragm is the muscle that separates your lungs and rib cage from your belly. When you contract your diaphragm, it moves downward, pushing your belly out and pulling air and oxygen into your lungs. If you push your belly out, making it pooch out as far as you can, you are using your diaphragm. When you breathe by contracting your diaphragm, it is called, unsurprisingly, *diaphragmatic breathing* or *belly breathing.*

Breathing this way, using your diaphragm rather than the muscles in your chest wall to expand your lungs and pull air into your body, creates a natural calming response in your body. When you belly breathe, you activate your parasympathetic nervous system (PNS), the part of your nervous system that is responsible for calming you by slowing your heart rate and lowering your blood pressure. Your PNS counteracts the stimulating impact of your sympathetic nervous system (SNS), the part of your nervous system that is in charge of activating your emergency alert system, making your heart pound and flushing your system with stress chemicals. When you are feeling stressed or on edge, or are having trouble quieting your mind for sleep, belly breathing can help.

Many people are natural chest breathers; they usually breathe in by using the muscles in their chest wall to lift the ribs and inflate the lungs. If you are a natural chest breather, belly breathing may be a bit challenging at first, but with practice you will get the hang of it.

To learn belly breathing, you first have to learn to breathe with your belly. Makes sense, doesn't it? It's easiest to do this lying on your back, but once you have the hang of it, you can do it sitting or standing as well. Read the instructions through first so you know what the plan is, and then find a comfortable place to lie down while you practice. If you'd rather listen to the instructions, go to http://www.kor umindfulness.org/guided-meditations and listen to "Koru Belly Breathing."

Instructions for Belly Breathing

Lie flat on your back on the floor or bed. Put one hand on your belly and one on your chest, and breathe normally. Pay attention to your hands, and see whether you can detect which one is moving more when you breathe in. Does the hand on your belly rise up toward the ceiling when you breathe in, or is the hand on your chest moving? If your chest hand is moving more, you are most likely a natural chest breather. If your belly hand is moving more, you are most likely a natural belly breather. It doesn't really matter, but if you are a chest breather, you may have to be a bit more patient with yourself as you learn this new skill.

Once you've gotten a clear picture of what is actually happening as you breathe your usual way, start trying to shift your breath so that when you inhale, the hand on your belly rises more. As you breathe out, the belly hand should sink back down as you release air. As you get more skilled at breathing with your belly, you'll notice the hand on your chest is relatively still compared to the hand on your belly, which moves gently up and down with your breath.

Once you think you have sorted out how to inhale by pushing your belly out, it's time to practice. Still lying down, place both hands on your belly, and if it feels comfortable, allow your eyes to close. Let your attention settle on your hands as they rest on your belly, and feel them moving up and down as you breathe. It *may help to imagine that your belly is a balloon filling with air as you breathe in.*

Your mind will probably wander after just a few breaths, but that is totally normal and no big deal. When you notice your mind has wandered, bring your attention back to the sensation of your hands resting on your belly, without judgment or criticism. Continue to practice pushing your belly up toward the ceiling with each in-breath, letting it float back down with each out-breath.

When you feel you are starting to get the hang of it, see whether you can deepen your breathing by counting slowly up to three with each in-breath. After a few minutes, experiment with deepening your breath even more by counting slowly up to four or five as you breathe. Continue in this manner until about ten minutes has passed.

If you are practicing belly breathing at bedtime, you may find that you fall asleep before your ten minutes is over. Don't fret about that; instead notice that you now have a skill that calms your body, quiets your mind, and allows you to slip into sleep. It's a nice way to end your day.

Once you have the hang of belly breathing, you can do it anywhere, anytime. Students often tell me that while they are seated at an exam, waiting for the test to begin, they will belly breathe to ward off any pretest jitters. Riding the bus home from school or work is a good time to practice this relaxing breathing as you release the stress that has built up throughout a busy day. Many people have told me that belly breathing prior to an important interview helped them stay calm and focused so they could perform their best.

Practice Tip: Having trouble figuring out how to breathe with your belly? Lie on the floor and place a tissue box on your belly. Concentrate on pushing the tissue box up toward the ceiling as you breathe in. See how high you can get it to rise on a nice, slow in-breath. Watch it sink back down as you exhale.

Dynamic Breathing to Energize and Clear Your Mind

Do you need to wake up so you can finish a project? Are you feeling so tense and anxious that it is just killing you, and there is no way to sit still and watch your breath? This next skill, called *dynamic breathing,* is just the ticket for times when you are tired and need reenergizing or are very anxious and need a way to refocus your energy.

It's a ridiculous-looking skill, and you have to be prepared to tolerate looking like a wild, flapping chicken for a few minutes to get the benefit of it. Please don't think you are too hip for this skill. I felt that way at first, and if my Koru codeveloper, Margaret Maytan, hadn't insisted that it was incredibly helpful, I would have missed out on one of the most useful tricks I know.

Dynamic breathing is a rapid, deep, and energetic style of breathing done standing up, breathing in quickly and deeply through your nose. It is important to KEEP YOUR MOUTH CLOSED while you do this, to avoid hyperventilation.

It is hard to learn this skill just by reading about it, but I've done my best to explain it below. The best way to learn it is to watch the video on dynamic breathing in the Koru app or at http://www.korumindfulness.org/guided-med itations.

Instructions for Dynamic Breathing

To get started, stand up and practice taking deep, sharp breaths in and out through your nose. It may help to emphasize the exhalation as you are getting used to it. Once you have the hang of it, add arm motions. Keeping your arms at your side, elbows bent, pump them up and down like bellows (or flapping wings) to help move the air in and out of your lungs. Your arms should pump down to your rib cage on the out-breath and up and out on the in-breath. The arms are strong and pumping, not loose and flapping, but you will still look like an agitated chicken—thus the common name for this skill, Chicken Breath.

To make things even more energizing, add movement in your legs, bending your knees in time with your breath. Bend your knees on the out-breath and straighten your knees on the in-breath.

It's a lot to coordinate at once, so take your time and go slowly until you get it figured out. When you feel like you've got it, gradually pick up the pace until your movements are brisk. Breathing in and out, pumping your arms and legs, you will become warm and your pulse will pick up. If you feel lightheaded, slow down and make sure your mouth is closed. Stop if you start to feel dizzy. Practice for a few minutes. Put on some fun drumming music to help you get into it even more.

After you stop, bring your attention to the sensations in your body for a few seconds. What do you notice? What is your energy like now?

This is a great mindfulness exercise, because it is hard to worry about anything else when you are occupied with coordinating all components of dynamic breathing. When you need an extra-powerful anchor to keep your attention in the moment, dynamic breathing can be your go-to skill.

Students tell me they use dynamic breathing when it is late at night and they still have seven pages to write of their ten-page paper.

Better than caffeine, dynamic breathing will both wake you up and calm you down. Once your work is done, you can readily get some sleep, unlike when you have relied on a caffeine buzz to stay awake.

So now you know two breathing exercises: belly breathing to calm your body, helping you relax and settle your mind, and dynamic breathing to energize you or clear out your mind when you are in a state of high distress.

The Body Scan to Practice Holding Your Attention in the Present

The body scan is a nice mindfulness practice to begin with as you start to learn the skill of focusing your awareness in a nonjudgmental way on the present moment. In this meditation, you bring your attention to body sensations, using the sensations to "anchor" your awareness on your present-moment experience.

If you are like almost everybody else, you will find that your mind frequently wanders away from your anchor, which is also known as the *object of meditation.* See whether you can notice when your mind has wandered, and without making judgments about yourself or your ability to do this, gently bring your attention back to the sensations in your body.

Remember, it is the nature of the mind to think, and you're not trying to stop the mind from thinking. You're just training your mind to stay grounded in the present by noticing when it has wandered away and gently bringing it back, over and over.

If you prefer to use a guided meditation, you'll find a free guided body scan at http://www.korumindfulness.org/guided-meditations.

Instructions for the Body Scan

Begin by getting into a comfortable meditation position, seated in a chair or lying on the floor. Warning: lying down for a body scan often leads to sleep, so if you want to stay awake for this, you may want to find a chair that comfortably allows you to sit upright, your feet resting on the floor. Let your hands rest in your lap, and allow your eyes to close. See whether you can keep your spine tall while your muscles relax around it.

Begin by bringing your awareness to the bottoms of your feet as you notice the feeling of your feet resting against the floor. Perhaps you notice pressure where your feet make contact with the floor, or the touch of your socks on your skin. Maybe you notice tingling or other sensations, or maybe you don't notice much sensation at all. It makes no difference; you are not trying to change anything, just to see what is actually happening in this moment.

As you continue to watch the sensations in your feet, allow yourself to become aware of your breath moving in and out of your body. If it seems helpful, try to imagine your breath moving in and out through the bottoms of your feet.

With each in-breath, allow your awareness to sharpen; with each out-breath, allow tension and tightness to be released from your feet. Breathing in, focus your attention; breathing out, release tension.

After a minute or so, move your awareness up to your lower legs. With an attitude of curiosity, see whether you notice any sensations in your shins or calf muscles. Can you feel your pants or socks touching your skin? Do you notice pulsations or tingles in your legs? Can you notice the muscles in your legs? Begin to imagine your breath moving in and out through your calf muscles, and with each in-breath sharpen your focus on the sensations; with each out-breath release tightness and tension.

If your mind wanders, see whether you are able to notice that your attention has shifted without judging yourself. You are seeing the nature of your mind at its most clear and natural when you observe the way your mind shifts, producing thoughts moving from one topic to the next. Bring your attention back to the sensations in your lower legs.

After a minute or so, move your attention up to your upper legs, your thighs. Again notice whatever sensations are present, and if it is helpful, imagine your breath moving in and out through the muscles of your thighs, releasing tightness and tension as you exhale, focusing your awareness as you inhale.

Continue moving slowly up the body in this manner, spending a few minutes on various body parts. After your upper legs, you can notice your hands on your lap, your arms, your back and shoulders, your neck, your jaw, the muscles around your eyes, and your forehead. Depending on how much time you wish to spend meditating, you can visit fewer or more places, spending just a few minutes at each spot, breathing in and out and noticing the sensations.

Before you finish, take a few moments to slowly scan your awareness through your body from head to toe. If you notice any areas of tightness or tension, let your awareness settle there for a few moments, breathing in and out through that tight place, and observing the sensations there. And again, when you notice your mind has wandered, just observe that. Allow yourself to be a curious scientist learning about how thoughts flow, rather than a punitive prison guard flogging yourself for moving outside the box.

Finally, settle your attention on your breath, watching the sensations as you take two or three slow, deep breaths before opening your *eyes. Take a few moments to stretch in any way that feels comfortable before getting up.*

Your Daily Practice

You now have four skills to practice: belly breathing, dynamic breathing, the body scan, and the simple breathing meditation you learned in chapter 2. Practice with at least one of these skills for ten minutes each day. If you are doing dynamic breathing, you can do that for just a few minutes and then finish up with a few minutes of one of the other skills.

Remember, this book is designed to help you conduct your own personal experiment into the benefits of mindfulness. As described in the introduction, your experiment will be more complete if you do the following things: Keep track of which skill or meditation you practice and how long you practice by logging it in a notebook or on the Koru app. Also, pick one of your daily activities, like washing your face or walking to class, to do with complete mindfulness each day. Finally, write down two things you are grateful for each day. Look back at the bulleted list in (see section titled "How to Use This Book") if you need a reminder about how to get the most from your personal experiment with mindfulness.

In the next few chapters, you'll learn more about working with your judgments and staying present-moment focused. The more you build your mindfulness muscle, the more real and meaningful these concepts will feel. So take your mind to the mindfulness gym, and practice one of your skills right now.

Chapter 4

Here Comes the Judge

You may remember that I explained mindfulness as a two-part proposition. The first part is about gathering your attention and holding it as best you can on the present moment. The second part is about cultivating a certain attitude, a nonjudging attitude. To achieve the full benefits of mindfulness, one must bring an attitude of calm curiosity, withholding criticisms and judgments, to the observations of the moment. In this chapter we are going to learn more about working with our mind's tendency to create judgments.

Trapped in Judgment

Most humans have the mental habit of dividing their experiences, automatically and immediately, into compartments of good, bad, and neutral. Without even noticing, you are probably going around habitually assessing and assigning value to virtually every thing/person/experience that crosses your path. These automatic assessments and assumptions lie at the heart of some of our most unhelpful biases, stereotypes, and self-imposed limitations.

Mindfulness practice allows us to start noticing all these assessments so that we can stop being controlled by them. That is what it means to cultivate a nonjudging attitude.

The problem with all these judgments is that they limit us. Because we don't typically notice them, they are often programs running constantly but unobserved in the background, controlling us without our awareness or consent. It's a bit like being in the movie *The Matrix,* living in a giant web of preconceptions that keep us from seeing the reality of our experience.

Every judgment or assumption you hold without questioning is a bar in a cage you are building around yourself. If you think without questioning, *I suck at this* or *I can't do this,* then you don't try and you don't grow. If you think without questioning, *He's a total loser* or *She's not my type,* then you limit your connections in life. If you think without questioning, *She's the only one who will ever love me* or *He's the only one who could make me happy,* then you stay stuck when you should let go. Each judgment is a limit you place on yourself or others. As soon as you see this truth, you begin to dismantle your trap. Learning to watch and release judgments during meditation is the precursor to seeing the judgments that constrain you during all the other moments of your life.

CONTEMPLATE THIS

Assumptions bind us to the past, obscure the present, limit our sense of what is possible, and elbow out our joy.

—Sharon Salzberg

No Point Judging the Waves

Sometimes we judge ourselves for having unpleasant emotions like jealousy or anger. This kind of judging just stirs yet another icky emotion—guilt—into our bitter emotional stew. The thing is, emotions in our minds are like waves in water. It is the nature of water to have waves. Depending on the weather, the waves may be huge and crashing or just little ripples, but there are always waves. You wouldn't criticize the water for making waves. No need to criticize your mind for doing its thing, either.

Finding the Judgments

The first step toward developing a nonjudging attitude is simply learning to spot judgments as they arise. To start, you can practice noticing judgments during meditation practice. For example, when you first begin to meditate, you will likely have thoughts such as *This is cool; I'm good at this* or *This is lame; what a waste of time.* These are part of the broad category of thoughts we call judgments.

Any thought about liking or not liking something or someone is a judgment. Any thought assessing whether something is good or bad, right or wrong is a judgment. Slightly less obvious judgments are opinions masquerading as statements of fact. *He's a loser. She's so hot. I'll never get this right. Anyone who believes that is an idiot.* These kinds of judgments are trickier to notice because we tend to believe they are "true" and do not see that they are really just products of our assumptions, biases, and mental habits. For example, Maria pointed out her uncertainty about the difference between opinion and fact when she said, "My ex-boyfriend is an asshole. I'm pretty sure that is a fact." Actually, it is just an opinion that she holds so strongly it *feels* like a fact.

Of course, not every thought is a judgment. Sometimes we plan for the future or recall something from the past, among other things. But most of us will have a heavy dose of evaluative thinking both when we are meditating and when we are not.

Dropping the Judgments

So developing a nonjudging attitude means first beginning to see judgments as they arise in their various forms and disguises. Then comes the tricky part: letting the judgment go without getting hooked by it. To let a thought go, you simply turn your attention back to the present by anchoring it on a physical sensation, like the feel of your breath. You don't have to force yourself to "stop thinking" or make decisions about whether it's a good thought or not (that's just more judging, by the way); you simply turn your attention away from it and let it move on by. This works when you are meditating and, with some practice, even when you are not.

Remember the metaphor from chapter 2 of our mind as a rushing river of thoughts? When you move your attention back to your breath, you have climbed back on the bank and the thought will have a chance to move on down the river.

For example, not buying into the story of *This is a waste of time* while meditating would mean recognizing the thought as a transient reflection of restlessness on your part rather than as an accurate assessment of the value of meditation. So, rather than ending your meditation session after sixty seconds because you think, *This is a waste of time,* you bring your attention back to your breath, curious about the next thought that will appear in the river.

It gets harder to let judgments move by without doing anything about them when the thoughts are about issues that seem more crucial. Opinions about who is right or wrong, or what your partner should not do or say, will pull you right into the river and you may be way downstream before you catch yourself. Fortunately, it doesn't matter how far down the river you float. You can always get back on the bank.

The point here is not that you should never form opinions. Obviously, we make necessary judgments all the time. We wait to drink our coffee because it is too hot. We don't buy a new computer because it is too expensive. But if you are making important life decisions based on strongly held perspectives that you are not even aware of, then you are vulnerable to being controlled by your unconscious biases.

Being Judicious with Judgments

How do you know which judgments are useful and which ones are just more "blah blah" floating between your ears? I like to distinguish between *observations* and *judgments.* Observations reveal truth; judgments conceal truth. Observing without judging is a great skill to learn and one that builds with the practice of mindfulness meditation. However, we are so used to making judgments that at first it can be hard to actually see the difference between judgments and observations.

An observation does not assume any inherent value; it more precisely illuminates how things are. For example, you might judge your coffee as "bad" rather than observing that it is cold. I'm not saying you have to like cold coffee, but I want you to see the way your mind quickly judges it "bad" rather than just observing the way it is.

Other examples: *I am fat* is a judgment, whereas *My body mass index is X* is an observation. *I'm lazy* is a judgment, whereas *My energy is low* is an observation. *This class sucks* is a judgment, whereas *I'm having a hard time keeping up in this class* is an observation. See the difference?

Notice that all the observations invariably lead to exploration and growth. Is a body mass index of X a healthy size for you? Do you feel healthy and well or not? If not, is there a sensible approach to working on improving your health?

Is your energy low when you don't sleep or exercise enough or when you drink too much? If so, are those things you want to change?

Is there a different way to manage the work required for the class? Do you need to get help? What are your options?

Observations reveal the content of your river of thought and point you toward insightful action. Judgments just keep you stuck.

Different Is Just Different

A common judging pitfall is the way most of us conflate "different" with "bad" or "wrong." Different is not bad; it's just, well, different. The automatic negativity we apply to the perception of difference is behind all of our biases, both conscious and unconscious. It takes practice to observe someone or something as different without automatically attaching some negative judgment to that observation. But the truth is that everybody is different. We have different likes, looks, priorities, and beliefs. If someone speaks a different language, has a different faith tradition, or pursues different goals than you do, it is not a criticism of either you or them. The automatic association of "different" with "bad" seems to me to be one of the greatest challenges for humans living in shared communities. Mindfulness can help you notice these automatic judgments so that you have a chance to consider them more fully without acting on them in word or deed. A little mindfulness can go a long way toward creating more tolerant and peaceful societies.

TAKE A MOMENT: Practice identifying your judging thoughts. Close your eyes and take a few breaths. Stay alert for any thoughts that emerge in your mind. If it helps, you can imagine each thought going by as a leaf in a stream or a package on a conveyor belt. Try to detect whether the thought has any quality of judgment to it: liking or not liking, or thinking something should change or stay the same. Then let it go and stay alert for the next thought. Stop after you've observed about ten thoughts.

Dismantling the Trap

It may sound hard to believe, but dismantling the judgment trap begins to happen spontaneously as you train yourself to observe and release judgments. I remember when I first began meditating I was surprised at the number of cynical, critical thoughts floating by in my head. I asked my teacher, Jeff Brantley, one of Duke's mindfulness gurus, what I could do to stop the negativity. I confess I was skeptical when Jeff advised me to trust the mindfulness and continue to patiently observe and release the critical thoughts. From my perspective, the problem was that the thoughts kept coming—not that I needed to get better at dismissing them. I wanted to *make* myself nonjudgmental so I could be sure I was doing it "right." Didn't I need to *do* something?

Though unconvinced, I persisted. To my surprise, just acknowledging the negativity without adding another layer of judgment on top (*I am a bad person for having all these judging thoughts)* seemed to turn down the flow. As if someone upstream was purifying the water at its source, harsh critical thoughts ceased to appear in my river as often. This all seemed to happen effortlessly as I persisted with my meditation practice.

Persisting with Your Practice

Effortlessly, that is, if you don't count the effort I put into developing my mindfulness practice. Now it's time to put a little effort into yours, keeping an eye out for your mind's tendency to make judgments. Take ten minutes now and do one of the four mindfulness practices we covered in chapters 2 and 3 (breath awareness, belly breathing, dynamic breathing, and the body scan).

Next, we'll explore what happens when you land in the present.

Chapter 5

Here You Are in the Present Moment

Darrin was a student athlete. He had injured his knee and was benched because of it. He had come to Koru to learn mindfulness to help him manage his physical pain, but also to deal with the emotional fallout of being unable to compete. In class one day, he talked about how learning to stay more present-moment focused was helping him deal with his injury.

As part of his rehabilitation, Darrin had been getting painful injections into his knee. He said, "I used to worry all week about these procedures. Lately I've been seeing that if I work on staying in the present, it's a lot easier on me. I can deal with the pain when it actually happens, but I don't need to be dealing with it now." His pain did not exist in the present moment, and he was choosing to stay right where he was, right there in the present.

Making Contact with the Present

Learning to completely inhabit the present moment is the key to developing the skill of mindfulness and experiencing its real power. Like the clear skies and smooth water in the eye of a hurricane, the present moment is a safe haven in a tumultuous life. Problems and worries may swirl around you, but when you are anchored in the present, you are less susceptible to being swamped by stress.

Your path out of the storm and into the calm center is through awareness of physical sensations. The entrance is hidden in plain sight; like a door you have to feel with your fingers to find, it becomes apparent when you connect with your sensory experience. Any physical sensation like touch, sound, or the feel of your breath can work to open the portal to the present moment.

In my experience, the access I have to stillness during a meditation period is directly proportional to the exclusivity of my attention on my breath. If my mind is restless and jumping around, I only skirt the surface and I feel less anchored in smooth waters. If my focus is adhered tightly to the breath, seeing the entire in and out, and the pause in between, I sink more fully into the protection of the present.

I don't want to give the impression that I have full control over this. A wide range of variables influences our ability to focus. External factors (noise, temperature) and physical factors (illness, fatigue, hunger) all impact our concentration. Mental factors are often the most challenging to work with: financial worries, relationship fears, self-criticism, planning for the future, old resentments, and many more distractions may arise. But as with anything else, the more you patiently and compassionately practice securing your attention to the sensation of your breath, the easier it becomes. Once you have the experience of using your breath to enter the present moment, you will have access to the vast expanse of calm, focused energy that resides there.

TAKE A MOMENT: Experience the difference between *thinking* about the present moment and *inhabiting* it. To inhabit the moment, close your eyes and take ten slow, deep breaths. As best you can, hold your attention on the sensation of the breath moving in and out of your body. Follow each inhalation from beginning to end. Notice the brief pause before the exhalation starts, then watch as the breath moves out. When your mind wanders, patiently bring it back. Be a curious scientist, aware of every changing sensation as your body breathes.

Sharing the Present with Painful Emotions

When the present moment contains a painful, intense emotion, your attention will quite naturally be drawn exclusively to the uncomfortable sensation; the discomfort completely fills your screen, making it hard to notice anything else. In those moments, it is helpful to zoom your attention out so that you can take in a fuller, more accurate view of the reality of the moment. For example, you may be feeling intense anger, but at the same time, your feet are grounded firmly on the floor, your breath is moving in and out of your body, there are sounds in the environment around you, and you can feel your shirt against your skin. Staying open to the totality of the sensations in the moment will help you stay balanced and grounded.

Expanding your awareness in this way allows you to open up and make room for the emotion. Zen master Shunryu Suzuki (1970) compared staying present with strong emotions to taming a wild bull. He said the best way to tame a wild bull is to secure it in a large pasture where it has plenty of space to move about. In a small or tightly controlled space, the bull will just become more agitated. Without any containment at all, it will run wildly away. A large enclosure keeps the bull in view while it thrashes and eventually settles on its own. Similarly with powerful emotions, if you try to control or suppress them, your agitation will likely increase. But if you observe them and give them space by expanding your awareness to include more of the details embedded in the present moment, they will eventually settle on their own, drained of their energy.

Flowing in the Moment

You may be familiar with, or perhaps have even experienced, a particularly potent type of present-moment engagement that is often referred to as *flow* or *being in the zone.* Athletes, musicians, and artists sometimes experience flow when they are deeply concentrated on their sport or art. The common elements of flow experiences are the feeling of complete immersion in the moment, the ability to achieve exceptional performance, and the presence of spontaneous joy.

In a state of flow you are wholly concentrated on your task; no other thoughts enter your mind. You feel challenged but fully able to meet the challenge. When flowing, one often has the sense that time has slowed; each moment seems full and clear. In this state athletic ability is optimized, and creativity is activated. Though you typically cannot develop flow at will, you can cultivate the mind state that allows you to enter into flow, and mindfulness practice is the most direct route to this state.

George Mumford (2015), an athlete himself and mindfulness coach to the likes of Shaquille O'Neal and Michael Jordan, talks about flow in his book, *The Mindful Athlete.* Mumford says, "The more you practice mindfulness, the more readily you set yourself up to experience conscious flow. Put differently, having a mindfulness practice is like watering your garden: it's the only way to make things grow" (73).

Science Note: Inhabiting the present moment can change your brain. A meta-analysis determined that there are eight regions of the brain that are altered by meditation practice (Fox et al. 2014). These brain regions are important in regulating emotions, improving memory, and increasing attention and awareness. Remarkably, this proves that we can alter the structure of our brain, improving its function in important ways, simply by learning to focus our attention in a particular manner. The authors observe that "one of the most interesting results to emerge from the nascent literature on brain structure and meditation is just how few hours of training seem necessary to induce neuroplastic changes" (65). In the same way that exercise can change both the appearance and the strength of our muscles, meditation can change both the structure and the effectiveness of our brains.

The Small Stuff, the Big Stuff, and the Good Stuff

In his book *The Power of Now,* Eckhart Tolle (2004) asserts that it is impossible to have a problem when your attention is fully in the present. He points out that your life happens only in the present moment. Problems and worries live only in the future or the past. In the present, situations occur that you manage in the moment, but they only become problems when you think about them with regret or worry.

Now, you may want to argue that you cannot avoid all your troubles just by staying present, and to some extent that is true. But here's the deal. Some of what seems like trouble is really just strong emotions such as anxiety, sadness, or anger. You might not enjoy the experience of these uncomfortable feelings, but they are not necessarily problems. You can use mindfulness to learn to ride through them with less distress.

Additionally, many of your troubles, including the experience of strong emotions, are only troubles when you think of them in the *future* with dread or the *past* with regret. For example, Rachel talked about how stressed out she feels when she thinks about all the work she has ahead of her during the course of a semester. It feels like an overwhelming problem when, from her seat in the *present,* it appears to be a giant wave of work that will bury her alive in the near *future.* She said that when she learned to focus on just one thing at a time, solving one problem at a time, completing one assignment at a time, she quit dreading the work. It became a series of manageable tasks that got done, with her full attention, one moment at a time. No big deal.

Of course you will be able to call to mind all manner of horrible, scary, or heartbreaking moments that could overwhelm even a person well-anchored in the present, but most of the "troubles" we deal with on a daily basis (parking tickets, broken zippers) are not those kinds of disasters. A very popular series of books from the 1990s about stress management illustrates this well. The title of each book started with *Don't Sweat the Small Stuff,* and the first title in the series befittingly ended with ... *And It's All Small Stuff* (Carlson 1996).

Though most of our day-to-day struggles will generally qualify as "small stuff," unfortunately, we will all face some misery at some point in our lives. Part of the reality of being human is that sometimes we fail, we get sick, we have accidents, we lose people we love. We will have moments in our lives in which we have no choice but to tolerate pain.

Can you imagine, though, letting this pain live only in the moment of its origin, not dreading its future occurrence or revisiting it in the past indefinitely? If you can corral these most painful experiences in the moment they occur, they lose their power to control your life. It is when you look with dread toward them or are unable to leave them behind, for one reason or another, that they can cause distress far beyond the borders of their existence in time. I'm not suggesting this is a simple thing to do; none of us can easily get past deep, painful wounds. But you can use meditation practice to help you move in the direction of greater peace of mind.

TAKE A MOMENT: Reflect for a moment on whatever it is that is bothering you these days. Is it something that is actually happening right now, something that you are worrying about handling later, or something that is already over and done? Can you, like Darrin did with his knee injury and Rachel did with her schoolwork, begin to take your day one moment at a time, dealing with any challenges as they come?

Simple but Not Easy

Learning to inhabit the present moment is a powerful way to manage difficulties when they occur and to experience fully the more delightful moments of your life. It is excellent news that we can reduce our experience of suffering, even if only to a small degree, by staying more present-moment focused. However, it is important that you don't turn this bit of knowledge into yet one more whip you flog yourself with *(I've got all these problems and I'm bad at present-moment awareness, too).* The skill of staying present takes constant practice. I practice every day and still have plenty of mindless moments, lost in angst about some feared future event that might not even happen *(If I don't get over this cold by Monday, I'm going to have a really tough day at work).*

Over time, though, I've gotten better at it, and I live with greater ease than I used to. You can do this too if you are willing to work at it with an open mind, not criticizing yourself when you don't find it easy to stay permanently present. Fortunately, we are not limited in our lives to doing only the stuff that is easy. What would be the fun of that?

In the next chapter, I'll introduce you to your observing mind, the part of your mind that handles awareness. But before moving on, take ten minutes to practice one of the mindfulness skills we covered in chapter 3 (belly breathing, dynamic breathing, the body scan). If you are particularly tired or restless, practicing dynamic breathing for a few minutes will energize you and help steady your mind.

Chapter 6

Meet Your Observing Mind

Though it is probably overly simplistic, I like to say that we have two mind modes, *thinking mind* and *observing mind.* Cognitive scientists have a more refined way of distinguishing between various mind states, but for the purpose of learning meditation, I find thinking mind and observing mind to be useful descriptors. With meditation practice we are developing the power of our observing minds.

Thinking mind keeps your schedule, solves math problems, reorganizes your desk drawer, and makes all manner of decisions and plans. It is a very useful part of your mind, and in most Western cultures, it tends to be the dominant mind mode. Observing mind, on the other hand, inhabits the present moment by watching the flow of thoughts and sensations as you go through your life. In thinking mind, you are caught in the river of thought. In observing mind, you are sitting on the bank, watching the river flow.

Observing mind is that part of your mind that develops *awareness.* In fact, observing mind is sometimes referred to as *pure awareness.* Awareness is not quite thinking, though it makes use of thinking. Jon Kabat-Zinn (2005), the person probably most responsible for bringing mindfulness into the mainstream in the US, says, "Awareness is more like a vessel which can hold and contain our thinking, helping us to see and know our thoughts as thoughts, rather than getting caught up in them as reality" (93).

Observing mind, or awareness, is sometimes compared to the open expanse of clear, blue, unchanging sky. Thinking mind and emotions are more like the clouds and weather, constantly changing. Sometimes big storms blow in and dark clouds appear, momentarily obscuring the clear sky above, but the sky is there, arcing over everything. The vast observing mind holds everything; it is spacious and endless. You tap into observing mind when you bring your awareness to your present-moment experience.

Observing mind sees thoughts but doesn't follow them. It sees the struggle, but doesn't weigh in and pick sides. Observing mind knows what you feel, but neither judges nor fuels those feelings. It just watches, which is why Russell Simmons (2014), hip-hop mogul and meditation teacher, calls it The Watcher.

CONTEMPLATE THIS:

There is a difference between watching the mind and controlling the mind. Watching the mind with a gentle, open attitude allows the mind to settle down and come to rest. Trying to control the mind ... just stirs up more agitation and suffering.

—Henepola Gunaratana

Responding Instead of Reacting

One difference between thinking mind and observing mind is that thinking mind tends to be very reactive, whereas observing mind is more responsive. If you feel angry, it is your thinking mind that creates the story around the emotion. Your thinking mind tells you, very convincingly, *I can't believe that she thinks I am not pulling my weight on this project. She is so selfish. I'm the one who is carrying this team. I'm going to tell her what I really think.* In reaction to a strong emotion, thinking mind is ready to "help out" by rationalizing, blaming, and coming up with a plan of attack.

Observing mind sees the reactions but doesn't get caught up in them and doesn't assume they are "true." Observing mind notices the strong feeling of anger that erupts when you feel criticized. It notices where that feeling lives in the body. It sees that thinking mind is really believing the story it is telling.

Observing mind sees the impulse to *tell her what I think* while it also watches the breath, creating some space between the impulse and the action. This space allows enough time for you to create a more reasoned response, rather than a hasty reaction. Observing mind is a powerful component of wise action, allowing you to base your choices on careful observation of the present moment.

Strengthening Your Observing Mind

In most Western cultures, observing mind tends to be pretty wimpy, like a muscle that has never been exercised. Until you get some practice, your observing mind may have a hard time standing its ground when thinking mind is running the show. Just as muscles get stronger and more capable when you exercise them, your observing mind gets more powerful with exercise, too. Meditation, of course, is the best exercise of all for observing mind. Once you have been practicing for a while, you will be able to access observing mind even in tense situations.

Practice Tip: When you are meditating by using your breath as your anchor to the present moment, keep observing mind active by saying *in* and *out* silently to yourself as you breathe. This will help you gently tether your awareness to your breath. Keep alert for movements of the mind that draw your attention away from the breath.

Observing the Mundane and the Magical

A well-developed observing mind can transform some of the more mundane or even irritating experiences in life. For example, sometimes when it is my turn to do the dishes, I feel very grumpy about it, particularly if it is at the end of a long day of work and I am tired.

While I am standing in the kitchen doing the dishes, I might be thinking, *Why do I have to do the dishes again? It's not fair. I do everything around here.* If I am checked out, indulging my thinking mind's complaints, I can be in a pretty foul mood by the time the dishes are done, filled with self-pity, believing the story my thinking mind is telling me and nursing resentment toward my unsuspecting family members.

However, if observing mind kicks in, my perspective on the task changes completely.

Instead of being lost in grumpy thoughts about the chore, I turn my attention to the pleasant feel of warm water on my hands, the scent of the soap bubbles, the clink of the dishes as I load them into the dishwasher, and the motion of my arm as I wipe down the counters.

In truth, there is nothing unpleasant about the experience of washing the dishes at my house. It is mostly full of pleasant and neutral sensations. I don't have to do anything painful like scrape the plates with my fingernails or poke myself with the knives. If observing mind can hold me in the present moment, in contact with the *reality* of my experience, then at the end of the task I feel relaxed and cheerful, ready for whatever is next.

Wonderfully, observing mind also enhances your experience of the more pleasurable moments of your life. In fact, for me, this has been the best part of developing a more capable observing mind. Observing mind takes in beauty and pleasure with perfect clarity.

Have you ever been so overcome with pleasure at a particular time that you thought, *This moment is perfect!* or *I hope I remember this moment forever?* Those thoughts reflect perfect mindfulness, your observing mind taking note of all that is wonderful in the moment. As your observing mind gets stronger, you will start to notice even more of the pleasurable moments of your life.

Have you ever looked forward to an event with great anticipation and then found you didn't enjoy it as much as you expected? Often that's because thinking mind has pulled you out of the experience, robbing you of the anticipated pleasure. Tiffany told her Koru class how her observing mind had salvaged an important event for her. She said, "It was my twenty-first birthday and my friends had planned this great dinner party for me. We were sitting around the table having this amazing meal and I noticed that I wasn't enjoying myself. I was worrying about whether everyone else was having fun and thinking about how maybe things could be better. I was totally ruining it. When I realized I was lost in my head, I remembered to turn on observing mind. I looked around the table at each person's face, I heard all the laughter, and I really tasted my food. Almost immediately I felt this rush of good feeling. It was so great to really be there, instead of off in my head missing the party."

Observing mind will do this for you—make sure you show up for the good times. Your life will have many awesome moments; wouldn't it be great to register with clarity every single one of them?

TAKE A MOMENT: To give your observing mind a workout, pick a chore that you do most days—maybe the dishes, the laundry, or tidying up. Next time you start that chore, turn up your observing mind. Notice all your physical sensations by checking in with each of your five senses: touch, taste, sight, smell, and hearing. If any thoughts or emotional responses come up, just notice them and then turn your attention back to your physical sensations in the moment. See if you can maintain this level of awareness until the chore is complete. When you are finished, check in with yourself; notice how you are feeling in that moment and whether your experience of the chore was different when you did it with full awareness.

Staying the Course

In the next chapter, I'll review some of the obstacles that you are likely to meet as you continue with your experiment in living mindfully. If you have been diligently working on your personal experiment with mindfulness, then you have probably encountered one or more of these hurdles already. Developing your observing mind is an important part of working with challenges, so do your ten minutes of mindfulness practice now, and then read on to find out how to manage the obstacles that are sure to arise.

Chapter 7

Overcoming Obstacles

By now, you may be a week or more into your experiment with mindfulness and meditation. Maybe you are loving every minute of it. Or maybe not.

Actually, it is very likely that you have stumbled across a roadblock or two. Pretty much everyone does. I sure did, and I still do on a regular basis.

Traditional Buddhist teachings on meditation identify five obstacles, called *hindrances,* to meditation. These five hindrances can get in the way of developing a meditation practice in the first place, and they can keep you from persisting when things get challenging. If not identified and worked with, the hindrances will bring your progress to a halt.

The five traditional hindrances are greed, aversion, sloth or torpor, restlessness or worry, and doubt. You can recognize the traditional hindrances in the challenges that my students say they struggle with when they are learning meditation: sleepiness, restlessness, skepticism, procrastination, and time pressure.

Obstacles and Antidotes

It's useful to have some awareness of these typical challenges, as well as some strategies for working with them. Let's take a look.

Sleepiness

Obstacle: New meditators often say that they fall asleep every time they try to meditate. In Koru class, it is common for students to doze off during the meditation practice. I am a big fan of sleep, and in my experience most young adults do not get enough of it. So if you fall asleep every time you sit down, your body may be telling you that you need to sleep more. Take a look at your sleep patterns and see if this is true. Are you getting seven to nine hours of sleep most nights? If not, you might want to address that first.

Antidote: Sleeping is great, but it is not, in fact, meditating. If you fall asleep every time you sit down to meditate, then don't sit down. There are other ways of building your mindfulness muscle. Try an energizing mindfulness exercise such as dynamic breathing either alone or as a lead-in to your meditation practice, or a moving meditation such as walking meditation, which you will be learning in chapter 8.

Sometimes applying intellectual curiosity to the phenomenon of sleepiness will provide you some alertness. Try getting very curious about the sensation of sleepiness. How can you tell you are sleepy? Where do you feel it in your body? What are the sensations of sleepiness?

If you still find yourself nodding off, you might consider these other tricks: try meditating while standing up, meditating with your eyes open, or holding your breath for as long as you can. That last one may seem a bit harsh, but it will wake you up.

Restlessness

Obstacle: If you are like I was when I started meditating, you may find that sitting still and watching your breath is almost unbearable. Restlessness can make your mind race and your body ache to move.

I still vividly recall (it was that uncomfortable) my experience of intense restlessness the first time I sat with a meditation group for a thirty-minute meditation. It had to be the longest thirty minutes of my life. My thoughts went something like this: *How long have we been sitting? I'm sure we have been sitting here for longer than thirty minutes. This is miserable. Why am I even here? I wonder why that lady hasn't rung the bell yet. What if she is asleep? Maybe I should go wake* *her up. What if she has died? Will we all just sit here forever? What is wrong with these people? Oh my God, I can't take this anymore. If she is not dead, then I am going to kill her if she doesn't ring the f***ing bell!*

That, my friend, is what restlessness looks like.

Antidote: As noted above, you don't have to sit still to practice mindfulness. You can use dynamic breathing or walking meditation if you like. Or you can try a more calming meditation like belly breathing; using your belly to take slow, deep, breaths can reduce the mental and physical restlessness you feel. To anchor a very busy mind, use the gatha meditation, which I will introduce in chapter 8.

On the other hand, so far as I know, no one has ever died of restlessness. Even though I have felt that my head would explode if I had to sit still for another minute, it never actually did. Keep in mind that meditation is not about learning to avoid discomfort. In fact, the opposite is true. Meditation is about learning to hold discomfort in the great spaciousness of observing mind. We can watch discomfort, giving it room to move, while ceasing to fear and accommodate it. If you always avoid your restlessness by keeping your meditations very short or never sitting still, you will deprive yourself of the important lessons that restlessness can teach you.

So instead of always trying to find a way to meditate that doesn't incite restlessness, try being curious about it when it happens. What does restlessness feel like? Where do you feel it in your body? When you get to the point at which you know you will surely die if you sit still for another second, what happens if you take three more slow, deep breaths?

By the way, restlessness does eventually go away. These days I can sit quite comfortably for long periods without feeling like I am going to explode.

CONTEMPLATE THIS:

The mind is likely to give up before the body does.

—George Mumford

Skepticism

Obstacle: Skepticism about this whole mindfulness business is typical among twenty-somethings. Here are commonly expressed doubts about mindfulness and meditation:

"There's no way meditation can do what everyone says it will do."

"Mindfulness might work for some people, but it won't for me."

"I'm not the sort of person who could ever meditate."

"I doubt I'd follow through with it, even though I think it probably would be helpful for me."

"It probably is useful, but I don't think it is the best use of my time. I'm so busy, it feels more useful to use the extra time to study or get through my e-mail."

"My mind is so busy, this meditation isn't really helping me."

Do any of these sound familiar to you?

Antidote: Rather than act on your skepticism, either by fighting against it or by giving in to your doubts, try to notice your doubts with your observing mind. All of these doubting thoughts are simply words or images floating by in the river of your thoughts. If your observing mind watches them, you will realize that you don't have to do anything about them. You will discover over time whether mindfulness serves a useful purpose in your life. During your exploration of mindfulness you will have all sorts of thoughts, and not just doubting ones. When you make some progress in your practice, you may even have some unrealistically exuberant thoughts (like *This mindfulness stuff is going to eliminate all stress from my life! Awesome!*).

Learning to see all manner of thoughts go by in the river of your mind without following the impulse to act on them is one of the great benefits of mindfulness. Your skeptical thoughts provide you with an opportunity to practice this skill. Notice the thoughts and let them move on down the river as you sit in meditation, waiting for whatever might come floating by next.

Procrastination

Obstacle: Sometimes the hardest part of meditating is getting started. Every meditator I know struggles with this. You want to do your meditation, you really do, but you never seem to actually get to it. Maybe you have the time, but you don't *feel* like meditating right at the moment. "I'll do it later" becomes your game plan, and before you know it, the day is over and you are too tired to meditate before crashing into sleep for the night.

Antidote: Most people find that once they get started, finishing the meditation is doable, but getting started can be as hard as pulling teeth.

If you can't make yourself sit down, then don't make yourself sit down! If you notice yourself not feeling it when it is time to meditate, just stop where you are. Take a couple breaths. Get as curious as you can about that feeling of not wanting to meditate. Where is it in your body? Does it change as you watch it for a few breaths? What thoughts are associated with the feeling?

Now look what has happened. You just tricked yourself into doing your meditation practice. You are standing there using your observing mind to monitor the thoughts and sensations you are experiencing in the moment. Stand there for a few more minutes and you will have completed your whole practice. Or maybe at this point you feel more inclined to sit down for a bit while you continue to watch your breath. Either way, being curious about the obstacle helps you move through it.

Time Pressure

Obstacle: "I'm too busy; I don't have time to meditate." Want to guess how often I have heard that one? And of course it is true; most young adults are very busy, going to school and/or working long hours. Additionally, when we feel stressed, we often feel *time pressure,* the sense that we don't have enough time to do all the things we need to do.

Antidote: I am sympathetic to the feeling of time pressure that you may frequently feel. Truly, I am. At the same time, I have yet to meet anyone who in actuality does not have ten minutes in a day to spend on developing awareness of her present-moment experience.

The trick is to find the time. Can you get up ten minutes earlier in the morning? A few minutes of quiet contemplation in the morning is a great way to start the day. Do you ride the bus or subway to school or work? If so, you could take ten minutes during your commute to practice mindfulness. What about at lunch, or first thing when you get home at the end of the day? How much time do you spend on Netflix, engaged in social media, or playing computer games? Can you salvage ten minutes there? How about taking ten minutes to meditate as part of your cooldown at the gym?

Conduct an honest appraisal of how you spend your day, and see if you can find a pocket of time you can use for meditation. If you absolutely cannot find the time, you might get curious about whether the feeling of *I don't have time* is actually a manifestation of skepticism *(I'm not sure it is* worth *my time)* or procrastination *(It's not how I* want *to spend my time).* If so, try the antidotes suggested for those obstacles.

Practice Tip: Having a regular schedule for your meditation will go a long way toward supporting a daily practice. Pick a time of day and a quiet place to meditate. For example, you might commit yourself to sitting in your living room every evening after dinner. Set a reminder so you don't forget, and do your best to stick with your plan.

If a few days go by and your plan is not working for you, then make a new plan and try it for a while. See whether a different time of day or different location makes you more likely to follow through.

Watch out for any tendency to be constantly changing your plan; no time will be perfect, and at some point you just have to make it work.

Over the Obstacles

Now that you are armed with awareness of the obstacles you are likely to face and strategies for getting around them, it's time to learn a couple more mindfulness skills for you to practice; that's what we'll do in the next chapter. Oh, and if you haven't done your ten minutes of practice today, now is always a good time.

Part 3

Expanding Your Understanding

Chapter 8

Mindfulness for Restless Bodies and Minds

If you have been practicing the skills we've already covered—breath awareness, belly breathing, dynamic breathing, and the body scan—for a week or more, it's time to try out a couple more mindfulness practices. In this chapter you will learn two more techniques: walking meditation and gatha meditation. Both of these practices are helpful when your body or mind is restless and focusing your attention is particularly hard.

I'll take you through both of these skills below, but if you prefer to listen to recorded versions, you can find them in the Koru app or at www.korumindfulness.org/guidedmeditations.

Moving While You Meditate

Except for dynamic breathing, the mindfulness skills and meditations you've learned so far involve sitting still and focusing your attention on your breath or body sensations. Sometimes, though, you are either too sleepy or too restless to effectively focus your mind while sitting still. Walking meditation is an easy-to-learn moving meditation perfect for those occasions.

Walking Meditation

Walking meditation involves walking slowly back and forth in a room or on a short path while you meditate. Instead of using your breath as an anchor, you focus your attention on the sensations in your feet as you take each step.

As with other forms of meditation, you can be sure your mind will wander. The remedy is the same: when you notice your mind has rambled off, simply turn your attention back to the sensations in your feet.

Typically, walking meditation is done very slowly; you'll probably walk at a slower pace than you have ever walked before. The word "zombie" may come to mind the first time you try this. The slow pace allows you to detect each sensation as you shift your weight, contract and relax your muscles, and move your feet forward.

I'm often asked if walking mindfully to class "counts" as walking meditation practice. Walking mindfully is an awesome habit to get into, but it's not exactly meditating. With mindful walking, you have a destination in mind, but you keep your attention on the sights, sounds, and sensations along the way. When doing a walking meditation, you have no destination in mind. Your only purpose is to enter into a meditative state, using the sensations in your feet as your anchor to the present moment.

Instructions for Walking Meditation

Find a place where you can walk unobserved. You need a clear path in a room or outside where you can walk in a straight line for a short distance. Take off your shoes if you want. Stand with your weight balanced evenly on both feet. Let your arms hang relaxed by your sides, or clasp your hands comfortably behind your back. Let your gaze rest on the ground in front of you.

Bring your attention to your feet and prepare to begin walking forward. As you slowly lift your right heel, then the ball of your right foot off the ground, notice every sensation. Swing your foot forward, placing it on the ground and feeling your weight shift onto the right foot, as your left foot now begins to lift and swing forward. As you place your left foot on the ground and shift your weight forward, notice your right heel now leaving the ground, and so on.

Keep walking at a slow pace, holding your attention on your feet and paying exquisite attention to every movement, every shift of weight. Be intensely interested in all that is involved in every step.

Notice when your mind wanders, and without judging yourself or your wandering mind, bring your attention back to the sensations in your feet.

When you've gone a short distance or get to the end of the path you selected, come to a stop with your feet grounded directly below your hips. Slowly turn around to face the opposite direction, observing carefully the weight shifts and movements necessary to turn your body. Stand for a moment, noticing sensations in your body, and then begin walking back along the path you have just come down, slowly and attentively.

Walk back and forth, continuing the meditation for at least ten minutes. Try moving at different paces, either slightly slower or quicker, and observe how your focus changes at different speeds. To end the meditation, stand still and observe your entire body as you take a few breaths.

Some people find that they love this meditation because it is easier for their awareness to stay anchored on the sensations in their feet than on the subtle feeling of their breath. Others notice feeling frustrated at the slow pace. Remember, feeling frustrated is not a problem; it's a great opportunity for you to learn more about how you react to frustration.

Regardless of your initial experience, please give walking meditation a fair try, practicing with it a number of times. Walking meditation is one of the fundamental mindfulness meditation practices, and there is much to be learned from watching your mind as it reacts to this different type of meditation.

Practice Tip: Need to infuse some energy or interest into your meditation practice? Take it outside. There's something about being in nature that enlivens your awareness and invites wonder. The sound of birds and the sensations of sun and wind on your face are great anchors to the present moment. Walking meditation done barefoot on soft grass or a sandy beach connects you with the present and the wonder of the natural world. My favorite place to meditate is in the tree house in my backyard. See if you can find a spot in nature to make your special meditation space.

Antidote to an Overly Active Mind

A gatha, popularized in this country by the Vietnamese monk and meditation teacher Thich Nhat Hanh, is a collection of phrases that you repeat to yourself while you meditate. Gathas are helpful for steadying a hyperactive mind, anchoring it a bit more tightly to the otherwise subtle sensations of your breath.

When your thinking mind is wildly busy, running in circles, it may feel like a high-strung puppy bouncing off the walls in a small space. Your observing mind has a hard time getting any traction at times like this. Reciting a gatha silently to yourself is like tossing your puppy a bone; your thinking mind settles in one place, making it easier for your observing mind to keep track of it.

Sometimes the students I teach are skeptical when they first hear about how the gatha works, but those same skeptical students often tell me that the gatha becomes their go-to practice for strengthening their observing mind when their thinking mind has run amok. Do your best to stay open-minded and observe objectively what happens as you work with the gatha.

Gatha Meditation

Working with a gatha can seem a bit complicated at first; bear with me while I explain how it works.

The gatha we teach in Koru is an adaptation of one that Andrew Weiss (2004) adapted from Thich Nhat Hanh. Read this gatha a few times to commit it to memory. Once you are used to the way a gatha works, you can search for different ones online or write one of your own, if you like.

> I know I am breathing in. *(In)*
> I know I am breathing out. *(Out)*
> I calm my body and mind. *(In)*
> I smile. *(Out)*
> I dwell in the present moment. *(In)*
> I know this is a precious moment. *(Out)*

Instructions for Gatha Meditation

To start, sit either in a chair or on cushions on the floor, with your back upright and tall, but not stiff. Set your meditation timer for at least ten minutes. Allow your eyes to close, or direct your unfocused gaze toward the floor. Find your breath in your body and watch it as it flows in and out. Begin reciting the words of the gatha silently to yourself, linking the phrases to your breath. So as you breathe in, you say silently to yourself, I know I am breathing in. *And as you breathe out, you say* silently to yourself, I know I am breathing out. Breathing in, you say, I calm my body and my mind, and so on.

Go through the whole gatha, and then start again at the beginning, continuing to link the phrases to your breath, over and over. As with any meditation, your mind will wander at times. When you get distracted or forget some of the words, no worries. Just bring your attention back to your breath and start again at the beginning of the gatha.

After several minutes, if it seems that your thinking mind has settled, you can simplify the gatha by dropping down to just these words:

- In
- Out
- Calming
- Smiling
- Present Moment
- Precious Moment

So as you breathe in, you simply say silently to yourself, In. As you breathe out you say, Out, and so on. Go through the one or two words of the shortened gatha over and over as you continue your meditation, linking the words to the flow of your breath.

One more thing: when you say the words I smile or smiling, move your mouth into a slight smile. Most people notice subtle fluctuations in their mood when they smile. See if you do too.

Practice with the gatha until you can readily recall the words and have gotten the hang of it. Many people find that the gatha helpfully anchors their awareness on their breath. Stay curious as you work with it, resisting the urge to form any opinions about its usefulness until you get comfortable with the skill.

Science Note: Smiling decreases the impact of stress on your cardiovascular system and improves your mood. You may think that it is the other way around—when you feel happy, you smile—but it has been known for many years that putting a smile on your face, even a fake one, increases positive feelings like contentment and happiness.

Turns out that even a fake smile can do more than improve your mood. Scientists found that by forcing their subjects' faces into a smile by having them hold chopsticks (yes, chopsticks) in their mouths, they could reduce the cardiovascular impact of stress, even when the subjects were not aware they were smiling. So if you are looking for a simple stress management strategy, put a smile on your face, even a fake one. You and your heart will feel better (Kraft and Pressman 2012).

TAKE A MOMENT: Check in with yourself for a few moments now. Notice your level of motivation to try these new skills. Remind yourself about the reasons you became interested in learning mindfulness and started reading this book.

Your Daily Practice

You now have six skills to choose from for your daily mindfulness practice: the four you learned earlier in chapters 2 and 3 (breath awareness, dynamic breathing, belly breathing, and the body scan) and these two new ones (walking meditation and the gatha).

Though you don't need to be expert at all the skills you will learn in this book, it is important to try them all multiple times. As you practice, you will discover which ones resonate with you, and those will become your favorites. You will likely find that your mood and energy influence which skill seems like the best choice to practice on any given day. For example, walking meditation is perfect when you are restless and want to move your body while you practice focusing your mind.

You've made it quite a long way into your experiment with mindfulness by now. If you've gotten a bit slack about your daily mindfulness homework, look back (see section entitled "How to Use This Book") in the introduction for a reminder about recording what you're grateful for and staying mindful during one of your routine chores or activities each day.

In the next few chapters we'll explore how mindfulness helps you work with your thinking mind to reduce your stress levels, and then we'll look at the important concepts of grasping, acceptance, and resilience. The information will be more meaningful if you are accumulating experience with meditation, so take a few minutes now to try the gatha or walking meditation before moving on.

Chapter 9

Thinking Mind Is a Stress Machine

Now that we've looked at the basics of mindfulness, including how to anchor your attention in the present, develop your observing mind, and watch out for judgmental thoughts that trap you, it's time to explore how mindfulness can reduce suffering in your life.

To start, it's helpful to get better acquainted with the way your mind works and learn to recognize common thinking patterns that amplify stress. If you can identify and modify these thought patterns, you can improve your quality of life even if your life situation stays the same.

You may be dealing with hard realities: the need to work several jobs to pay the rent, heartbreak, trouble getting started with a new career, a heavy academic load, or the toxic effects of discrimination. Meditation can reduce the stress in your life, but not by magically making these hardships disappear. Even if you become the Supreme Ruler of All Meditators, these challenges will still be there. However, you can feel less burdened if you learn to approach these difficulties differently. It seems counterintuitive that your life can be better even if it is the same life, right? Let's spend some time pondering this idea further.

The Stories Your Mind Tells

Your life happens and your mind tells stories about it. For example, let's say you don't get an internship you had applied for. You will likely feel disappointed and anxious, which will set your thinking mind to work creating a story about it. (*I'm a total loser. I never get anything I want. Without that internship I've got no chance of getting a job I want in the long run.*) If you are intensely sad over a breakup, a different story shows up. (*I just can't keep a relationship. I always drive people away. I'll be alone forever.*) The story feels like an accurate description of your situation, but it really isn't; it's just your mind creating a scenario in reaction to your feelings in the moment.

Your mind's stories are only loosely based on facts; thus, you shouldn't believe everything you think. Because of a quirk of evolution known as *negativity bias,* your mind's stories, just like the evening news, prefer the drama of danger, disappointment, and shame. So if you just accept the stories without questioning them, it can seem like nothing good ever happens.

Negativity bias refers to our minds' natural tendency to tune in bad news and tune out good news. Evolution favored our ancestors who could spot problems and prepare for the worst-case scenario; thus, over time, humans got really good at it, becoming highly skilled at noting all things negative. This preoccupation with the bad, scary, and dangerous was useful for staying safe from predators on the savannah, but in the modern world it often fuels our day-to-day feelings of stress. By ignoring entirely all the neutral events of your day (getting dressed in the morning, riding the bus, walking to class) and only briefly registering the good things (hot coffee, sunshine on your face, your favorite song), your negativity bias makes it *feel* like you have more unpleasant moments than you actually do.

TAKE A MOMENT: Getting some perspective on your stories begins with getting skilled at recognizing that thoughts are just thoughts, ephemeral words or images generated by your mind that don't necessarily accurately describe reality. To begin seeing your thoughts more clearly, try this exercise, from a mindfulness-based form of psychotherapy called acceptance and commitment therapy: Write down or say aloud the next thought you have—for example, *I'm not having any thoughts.* (That's often the first thought you have when you try hard to notice a thought.) Next, put this phrase in front of the thought: *I am having the thought that* ... and say it aloud ("I am having the thought that I'm not having any thoughts"). Now do this for the next five thoughts you have. This seemingly silly exercise is an effective way to build your mindfulness muscle because recognizing your thoughts as thoughts takes practice.

Amplifying the Negative

Our negativity bias increases our feelings of stress because it shapes the way we experience life in the moment, recall what has already happened, and anticipate what is coming next. It takes nonjudgmental, present-moment awareness to balance this bias.

Over-Attention to the Negative in the Moment

In any moment, there are many things happening in your environment: pleasant, unpleasant, and neutral. If your attention is focused like a laser on the unpleasant, your experience will seem unpleasant.

For example, imagine you are standing in line at the grocery store and the line has stalled. You focus your attention on the slow pace of the clerk and begin to think, *Geez, what is your problem? I'm going to be late. Come on, hurry up!* Immediately, you start to feel angry and stressed.

But what else is happening in that moment? Probably some pleasant sensations like the smell of freshly baked bread or the feel of your soft, warm coat. There are also neutral elements like the rise and fall of your breath and the weight of your purchase in your hand. The pleasant, the unpleasant, and the neutral are all happening at once; you get to choose where you direct your attention.

Focusing exclusively on the negative (the clerk is slow, you are afraid you will be late) is like taking a close-up of the factors that are unpleasant and create stress, leaving out the rest of the scene. If you zoom your awareness out to take in all that is happening in the moment, you get a more complete view that includes the pleasant and neutral elements as well.

From this wide-angle perspective, the negative bits are small pieces of a rich, diverse picture. Your irritation is still there, but it no longer fills your screen. Other sensations that are soothing or benign are pulled into your awareness, balancing your perception of the experience.

Bear in mind that taking the wide-angle view of the situation is not about denying or repressing your negative feelings. It's just about having a more complete and thus more accurate view of reality.

This is a small illustration of how your relationship to your experience determines your stress more than the experience itself does. How stressed you feel when you finally leave the store will in large part be determined by your ability to hold in your awareness the full picture of your experience as you wait in line. Remember, whether you are angst-ridden or not, the line moves at the same pace.

Looking Back: Nursing Resentments

When our minds discover something they don't like, they tend to hang on to it like a tick on a hound dog. This tendency causes us to cling to irritations and resentments, making the most of all the unpleasantness they produce.

There's an old story that illustrates this well:

Two monks, a wise older monk and his devoted student, were walking down a country road on a beautiful summer day. They came to a river where a recent storm had washed out the bridge. Standing by the river was a lame, old woman in great distress. She said to the monks, "Please, help me! I must cross the river, but I am afraid I will drown."

The older monk was touched by her distress and agreed to help her. He lifted her onto his back and carried her across the river. Placing her gently on the bank, he said farewell and continued along the road.

The younger monk walking beside his teacher became agitated. He said angrily, "You taught me that we should never touch a woman for any reason, yet you ignored that important teaching when you carried that woman. You should not have done that. You have made me lose faith in you and your teachings." The young monk's agitation increased as they walked. Unable to enjoy the beautiful day, his mind was filled with resentful, disapproving thoughts about his teacher.

After a long while listening to his student's anger and criticism, the wise teacher said kindly, "I left that woman on the bank by the river. Why are you still carrying her on your back?"

We are all carrying resentments that we could put down. Often they serve no purpose but to disturb our peace of mind. Letting go of resentments, particularly ones that reflect old, deep, painful wounds, is never easy. It takes self-compassion and patience to begin loosening our grip on these old hurts. However, the first step toward putting down our burdens is to begin to notice when we are carrying them on our backs. What resentments are you carrying?

Looking Ahead: Anticipating the Worst

It is very easy to get caught up in worry about bad things that might happen. This fear about an uncertain future is a frequent source of stress for young adults, because so much about your life is still up in the air. Worries about school, job, and relationship prospects can occupy the bulk of your attention, creating chronic feelings of anxiety and stress. Learning to anchor your attention in the present is the best way to combat worries about the future.

Stella told a story that illustrated her experience with this. As an English major, she was frequently expected to write long papers, an activity that created intense feelings of dread. When she needed to write she would sit, staring at her computer, thinking, *I hate this; I am never going to get this done. I'll probably fail the class and if I do, I won't be able to graduate on time. My parents are not going to keep helping me if I don't graduate. I could end up homeless.* Stella was so tormented by her worries that she felt miserable, unable to focus on her work.

While these scary stories were spinning through her head, what was actually happening in the moment? Stella says that when she writes she is usually sitting in a comfy chair, wearing comfy clothes, her fingers tapping lightly on the keyboard. She is not experiencing any pain. Or hunger. Or blood loss. Her actual situation is not physically uncomfortable or dangerous, and yet she feels miserable. The source of her misery is those worried thoughts about impending doom that have taken up residence in her mind.

After she'd been practicing mindfulness for a while, Stella found it easier to write her papers. When she noticed her mind catastrophizing about her future as a homeless person, she would bring her attention back to the present by focusing on physical sensations, particularly the feel of her body breathing and her fingers tapping on the keyboard. Once she was anchored in the present, her fears about the future receded, making room for her natural creativity to flow.

Practice Tip: When thoughts are pressing in during meditation, rather than struggle with them, see them as a curious parade of strangers that you are watching from a bench on the sidewalk. Each passerby is different—some silly, some menacing, some dull. You wouldn't hop up and try to stop a stranger you didn't like the looks of; you'd just let him pass and see who was coming along next. Try treating your thoughts the same way.

Thinking It Through

Though we can't control much in this world, we do get to choose how we direct our attention. Directing your attention into the present and expanding your awareness to include the full picture are effective strategies for combating your negativity bias and reducing your sense of stress. Practicing present-moment awareness during meditation will teach you to stay present and keep your cool when you need it most.

Chapter 10

Get a Grip on Grasping and Aversion

Our thinking mind's negativity bias underlies a few mental habits that can be particular troublemakers if left unchecked. In fact, these patterns of thought are the ones the Buddha identified as the source of all human suffering. Sounds menacing, doesn't it?

Grasping, Aversion, and Delusion

The Buddha was born about 2,500 years ago as Siddhartha Guatama in what is now Nepal. Born a wealthy prince, he eventually rejected his wealth and devoted his life to investigating the source of human suffering as well as possible solutions to it.

After years of meditation and reflection, he identified three habits of the human mind as the starting points for most suffering; these habits have been translated into English as grasping or craving, aversion or hatred, and delusion.

The Buddha observed that humans tend to be focused on either what we don't have but want (money, prestige, sex, a better grade, a better job) or what we do have but fear we will lose (money, prestige, a hot girlfriend, a good grade, a good job); this is all "grasping."

The flip side of grasping is "aversion"; that's when we focus on what we don't want (a painful feeling, a few extra pounds, work to do when we'd rather be partying, a lukewarm cup of coffee, a line to stand in). Between all this grasping and aversion, it is almost impossible to be happy and satisfied, constantly trapped between trying to get more of what we do want and less of what we don't.

"Delusion" is a bit harder to explain, and we won't be delving into it, but it in part refers to the fact that we misunderstand the source of happiness and suffering. Because we think we can make ourselves happy by getting everything in our world just so, we don't put our energy into working on the real problem—our minds' habits of grasping and aversion.

To be clear, it is not "bad" or "wrong" to want some things and avoid others. As a matter of fact, these habits of mind are universal, and thus normal; we all do them, all the time. And yet, if we could see them, and do them a bit less, we would be less troubled.

The Problem with Grasping and Aversion

The source of grasping and aversion is our minds' exquisite ability to identify how things could be better. What could be the problem with that? you might ask. That's the source of our species' success, right? It's why we have hot showers instead of cold, fiber instead of dial-up. All true, and yet if left unchecked, it is also the source of chronic dissatisfaction.

If you always identify how things could be better, then no matter what you have, it is not quite good enough. No matter what you get, it doesn't keep you happy very long. Corey laughed and said, "Oh yeah. I know that one. I was pumped about my seat at the game the other night until I saw Jonathan had a better one. Then I was like, *Man, wish I was closer.*"

I frequently see this play out in more painful ways. Denise said about being a student at Duke, "I was so excited when I was accepted, but now that I'm here, it seems like I spend all my time thinking I need to be smarter and thinner. I'm not happy like I thought I'd be." No matter how wonderful your situation, if you mostly think about how you are not smart enough or attractive enough, or how the whole situation could be better, you are not going to be able to enjoy yourself.

If you start looking for this always-wanting-something-better thought pattern, you may see that you do this regularly. Ever catch yourself thinking, *If only I didn't have to worry about _____, then this would be perfect?* Maybe your car isn't good enough or your grades aren't high enough. Maybe you have a boyfriend but want a sexier one. Maybe the weather is too hot or maybe it's too cold.

Of course, it is not necessarily a problem to want things to be different. Identifying what needs changing is useful, but focusing excessively on what needs to be different gets in the way of seeing all that is positive and worthy in your life.

CONTEMPLATE THIS:

To whatever degree we desire, to that degree we suffer.

—Henepola Gunaratana

Grasping Pulls You Out of the Present

When your mind is hooked into grasping and aversion, you believe that happiness is not possible until you get or get rid of the person, thing, or achievement that you are pursuing or avoiding. It's a future-focused orientation that neglects the value in your present-moment experience. It creates chronic dissatisfaction and forces constant striving. Paradoxically, constant, anxious striving may sabotage your longed-for end result.

George Mumford (2015), who teaches big-name athletes to be mindful, talks about what happens when we become overly focused on an outcome. He explains that when you try too hard to achieve something, you may set yourself up to fail, because "focusing too hard on winning can take your focus away from doing the things you need to do to achieve your desired result" (115).

In other words, you will win more often if you think less about winning and more about playing. Keeping your head in the game means paying attention to what is happening right now. Staying in the moment makes you ready to respond as best you can to each challenge as it occurs.

This is not only true in sports. You'll perform better in interviews, on tests, and even in the bedroom, if you know what I mean, if you keep your attention focused on what's happening *right now* rather than worrying about what you hope to achieve in the end. This may be why mindfulness practice improves scores on standardized tests and can mitigate the damage caused by stereotype threat. (See Science Note below.)

Wanting to win the game or get the job or ace the test is not the problem. The problem arises when you are so captured by the desired outcome that you cannot bring your attention fully into the moment and perform optimally with what is directly in front of you.

Science Note: Mindfulness can improve your performance by bolstering your cognitive abilities, including working memory, concentration, and reasoning skills. In addition, mindfulness can help performance by limiting a particular obstacle known as *stereotype threat.* Stereotype threat refers to underperformance that occurs when an individual fears he will confirm negative stereotypes about his social group, even if he doesn't believe the stereotype to be true. For example, if a negative stereotype is activated in a testing situation—with subjects hearing comments or questions that invoked stereotypes like "men are sensitive" and "religious people aren't good at science"—women will perform more poorly on math tests and in chess games, men will perform more poorly on tests of social sensitivity, and Christians will perform more poorly on tests of aptitude in science. Fortunately, mindfulness exercises can blunt the negative impact of stereotype threat (Weger et al. 2012).

Any of us can find ourselves burdened by a negative stereotype that can potentially interfere with our optimal performance. Though not a panacea for this problem, mindfulness has a role to play by helping us stay focused and do our best, in spite of it.

Goals Are Good

To be clear, letting go of an overfocus on the end result does not mean that you shouldn't have goals. Goals and plans serve useful functions. They help you organize your life and keep you pointed in the general direction you wish to head. There is a time for thinking about what you hope to achieve, and a time for bringing your attention into the present in pursuit of the goal. Approaching your goals mindfully allows you to find the right balance.

Meditation Promotes Balance

Because grasping and aversion are universal and natural, you are not going to eliminate them. Nor should you waste time and energy criticizing yourself for these normal thought patterns. However, you can diminish the disruption caused by your ceaseless desires by practicing mindfulness meditation. Meditation cultivates two important attitudes that balance your constant craving: non-striving and gratitude.

Non-striving

The antithesis of grasping, non-striving means doing your best to accept each moment as it comes, without trying to change or improve it in any way. Jon Kabat-Zinn ([1990] 2013) says that meditation is different from any other activity in that it cultivates the attitude of non-striving because it is a "nondoing" activity. It teaches you to be a human *being,* rather than a human *doing.*

You won't have to practice meditation for long before you get to work with your striving nature. You'll spot your grasping habit the moment you find yourself wishing your meditation was more relaxing or less boring or over altogether. Wanting to feel peaceful and relaxed (grasping) or not wanting to feel restless and distracted (aversion) is part of almost every meditation session. You cultivate non-striving by observing those thoughts and feelings without responding to them. Your observing mind watches without reacting to them, and they gradually diminish, both during your meditation practice and at other times as well.

Gratitude

Intentionally developing gratitude for the good things in your life is another way to combat the dissatisfaction bred by grasping. Meditation cultivates gratitude by training you to pay as much attention to what you have as to what you don't have. Remember the man I mentioned in chapter 1, the refugee who is living in relative poverty but who lives with satisfaction and happiness? He seems able to focus his attention on the good things he has in his life. Most of us, including me, have to practice that mind-set. We have to work hard at staying focused on the positive things in our lives or risk staying mired in misery. That's one reason that in Koru we ask you to write down two things every day that you can feel grateful for (see section entitled "How to Use This Book" if you need reminding about this practice). Keeping a gratitude journal balances your negativity bias, prompting you to notice the good along with the not-so-good. So if you have lost track of your gratitude journal, dig it out now and write down two things you are grateful for.

Science Note: Robert Emmons (2007) has spent his career researching gratitude. His work has shown that keeping a gratitude journal produces an astonishing number of benefits. Even just a few weeks of regularly writing down what you are grateful for makes you happier, healthier, more outgoing, more optimistic, and less lonely. Gratitude has a powerful impact on our relationships as well. Emmons says,

"People who kept gratitude journals reported feeling closer and more connected to others, were more likely to help others, and were actually seen as more helpful by significant others" (Emmons 2007, 44). Thus cultivating gratitude is a simple activity with a powerful payoff.

Persisting with Your Practice

A regular meditation practice teaches you to recognize your constantly churning desires and develop discernment about which ones are worth pursuing. It also helps you pursue your goals in a way that is more balanced and offers greater satisfaction. These seem like good reasons to spend the time it takes to build your mindfulness muscle. Remember, if you haven't meditated in a few days, you can start again today, right now. It's never too late to pick up your practice again.

In the next chapter, we'll learn about another thought pattern, one that leads away from suffering: acceptance.

Chapter 11

Acceptance Reduces Suffering

Much of life's pain comes from the disappointment of having your unceasing desires unmet. Truth be told, over the arc of your life, you will have breathtakingly wonderful experiences, but you will also have losses and failures. Your general wellbeing will be determined less by the number of great moments, and more by the way you manage the difficult ones.

The key to dealing with those bad things when they happen is acceptance. If grasping and aversion are about always wanting this moment to be better or different, acceptance is about making the best of each moment, just as it is. I know from experience that twenty-somethings aren't that keen on acceptance until they understand it better, so stick with me while I explain it.

Resistance Increases Suffering

When unwanted things happen, it's painful. When we resist our pain, we multiply our suffering. Meditation teacher Shinzen Yeung often expresses it as a formula:

Pain x Resistance = Suffering

Pain is what you feel when something difficult, unpleasant, sad, or scary happens. It is inevitable that we will all feel pain. Resistance is all the things you do to escape pain. Think of it as aversion on steroids. Complaining is also a form of resistance. The soundtrack of resistance might go like this: *It's not fair. Why does this always happen to me? It's not my fault. You should not have said that!* Unfortunately, resistance amplifies pain and extends its duration.

Acceptance Decreases Suffering

You can't avoid pain, but you can avoid amplifying it into higher levels of suffering by cultivating acceptance. Acceptance is the state of mind that sees the present moment just as it is. It allows you to feel pain or sadness or anger without making it worse.

Isn't Acceptance Just for Chumps?

To be clear, the kind of acceptance I am talking about does not require you to give up or be passive in the face of disappointments. There is nothing passive at all about acceptance. It is a highly active state of awareness that points you toward wise actions. Acceptance is not what keeps you stuck; acceptance is what carries you through.

Understanding What Acceptance Is Not

It is important that you have a clear understanding about what acceptance is and is not. Acceptance is not the same as liking, agreeing with, or passively resigning yourself to anything. Let's dig a little deeper into the differences.

Acceptance Is Not Liking

Santiago said, "My roommate keeps coming in late, making all sorts of noise. He wakes me up, never says he is sorry, and it really pisses me off. I've been trying to accept it, but honestly, I don't like it." Santiago was struggling with the common confusion between acceptance and approval. He doesn't need to like or approve of his roommate disrupting his sleep in order to accept it.

Accepting the behavior means recognizing reality. It means seeing clearly that it does indeed happen and what specific problems it causes for him. Once he is fully aware of this, he can be thoughtful about what, if anything, he wants to do about it.

Does his roommate know it bothers him? Does he want to talk to his roommate? If so, what is the best way to approach him about this? Would it make more sense to just buy earplugs? Or ignore it for a while and see if it goes away? Would just ignoring the problem create resentment that would damage the friendship?

Any of these explorations and options could produce a helpful resolution to Santiago's problem; none of them involve his liking it.

Acceptance Is Not Agreeing

Harathi told her Koru class, "My mom and I argue all the time about dating. She believes I should only date Indian guys. I'm just never going to accept that."

The kind of acceptance I'm talking about has nothing to do with Harathi agreeing to date only Indian men. What might make Harathi's situation better, though, would be to stop arguing with her mother about it. The first step in that direction would be for Harathi to accept that her mother is probably not going to change her mind about this. Also, she will have to accept that she doesn't like how it feels when her mother disapproves of her choices. Then Harathi can decide: is she willing to tolerate the discomfort of her mother's disapproval in order to have the freedom to date whomever she chooses? It's entirely up to her. Acceptance lets Harathi see that it's best to put her energy into managing her own reactions to her mother's disapproval rather than trying to change her mother's mind about cross-cultural dating.

Harathi doesn't have to agree with her mother; she can accept that they have different perspectives. She also doesn't have to hate her. You can learn to calmly, kindly, and firmly disagree with someone you love if you can accept her for who she is, rather than being mad at her for not being the person you wish she was.

Acceptance Is Not Passive Resignation

Clyde was involved in the protests that erupted in 2014 following the killings of a number of unarmed black men by police officers. He said to his Koru class, "If we all just go around accepting that this stuff happens, nothing will ever change. I don't agree with 'acceptance.'"

Clyde was confusing acceptance with what Eckhart Tolle (2004) calls passive resignation, a common point of confusion. Acceptance has nothing to do with giving up. Acceptance is never about going along with or being resigned to brutality or injustice of any kind. Rather, acceptance means that you acknowledge the reality of the injustice and then act with wisdom to effectively promote change. In fact, acceptance—seeing what is true—is essential to effective advocacy. Acceptance may allow you to see reality with greater clarity in order to develop more effective solutions. It might guide you to change your approach to a particular battle by helping you see that it is not the best way to win the war, but it doesn't mean that you give up on working for social justice.

If you are stuck in the mud, passive resignation leads to *Oh no, I'm stuck. Guess I'll be here forever.* Acceptance leads to *Okay, I don't like it, but I am stuck. Now what am I going to do about it?*

Acceptance Is Not a Decision

You don't *decide* to accept a situation. Acceptance is an *action.* It is the action of bringing your awareness into the present and acknowledging what is true in this moment. As soon as you pull your attention into the present and are willing to see what is true, you are practicing acceptance. When you acknowledge the reality of any moment, letting go of ideas about how things "should" be or how you wish they were, you are practicing acceptance.

Acceptance is the action that lifts you out of being stuck in *I don't like it* or *It's not fair* and onto *What is the most sensible move in this moment?*

Getting to Acceptance

Maxine told us she finally understood "that whole acceptance-reduces-suffering thing" after her computer crashed just as she was finishing a complicated project that was due the next day. She lost her entire report and could not recover it. She said,

I panicked and started crying. All I could think about was what a disaster it was.

Eventually, I started to realize that even though rewriting the report was a total nightmare, it was my only option. I could stay up all night crying about it, or I could accept that I had to start over and get going on it. So that's what I did. I spent a few minutes watching my breath to help me calm down. Once I calmed down, I remembered there were pieces of the report I could recover from elsewhere, and I just got to work.

Every now and then I would start feeling sorry for myself and think, *Why does this always happen to me?* Then I'd say to myself, *It is what it is,* take a deep breath, and keep typing. It did suck, but I got it done and in the end I was relatively calm about the whole thing.

Notice that Maxine never did decide to like her situation, but she didn't waste precious time and energy cursing her fate, either. She accepted it and kept moving.

CONTEMPLATE THIS:

Mindfulness meditation doesn't change life. Life remains as fragile and unpredictable as ever. Meditation changes the heart's capacity to accept life as it is.
—Sylvia Boorstein

Practicing Acceptance

I annoy my daughter when I say in response to her complaints, "Sounds like another opportunity to practice acceptance." That may sound flippant, but actually, any time you notice something not going your way, it is a great time to practice acceptance. Remember, you practice acceptance simply by acknowledging the truth of the present situation; you don't have to decide to like, agree with, or resign yourself to anything. You just have to see that it is what it is.

Whether it is a frustration like Maxine's lost report, something worse like being rejected by your graduate school of choice, or even worse, the death of a beloved parent, there are times when you simply cannot do anything to eliminate your pain. In those moments, you can be compassionately present with your feelings, be they irritation, shame, or great sadness, and try not to make your suffering greater by refusing to accept whatever painful truth you are facing. Because even the most painful moments are temporary, if you can be kind and patient with yourself, with time your suffering will decline as you become clear about how best to manage your difficulty.

Meditation Builds Acceptance

Acceptance is the antidote to grasping, and it develops as you practice mindfulness meditation. Each time during meditation that you observe yourself wanting something to be different and choose to bring your attention back to the feel of your breath, you are practicing acceptance.

While meditating, you may notice yourself wanting more of something, such as free time, or less of something, such as work. Maybe you recognize thoughts about how life isn't fair or something is not your fault. Those thoughts tell you that you are resisting something. When you notice yourself wanting something to be different or resisting something that is real, and you intentionally pivot your attention back to your breath, you are practicing acceptance.

If what you are wanting has a powerful emotional pull to it, like wishing your girlfriend hadn't ended the relationship, you will get the opportunity, over and over, to practice letting go of that particular stream of thought as you sit in meditation. As you practice the skill of acceptance repeatedly in meditation, you will be better able to draw on it at other times, when you need it most.

Practice Tip: If during meditation you notice thoughts coming up that are fighting or resisting something difficult, practice saying silently to yourself, *It is what it is,* and with patience and compassion bring your attention back to your anchor in the present, whether that is your breath while you are sitting or your feet as you are walking.

Acceptance definitely takes practice, and meditation is the best way to practice it. Take ten minutes and practice one of your mindfulness skills now.

In the next chapter we'll see how acceptance leads to resilience, an important quality for surviving your twenties.

Chapter 12

Resilience: Surfing the Waves with Style

One of the great things about meditation is that it is tricky, a bit hard to learn. Why is that great? Well, it turns out that a moderate amount of difficulty is actually good for you, particularly if you grow and learn from the challenging or stressful experience. To paraphrase Nietzsche, what doesn't kill you makes you stronger.

The ability to bounce back or plough through a difficult experience is known as *resilience.* Mindfulness helps you build resilience, in part because it exposes you to just the right dose of difficulty, and in part because it teaches you to take a more productive approach to life's inevitable challenges.

Stress Can Make You Stronger

Gil Fronsdal (2008) offers a helpful metaphor for thinking about the benefits of dealing with difficulty. Imagine two rowers crossing the same pond but on different days and in vastly different conditions. The first rower crosses on a gloriously calm day. She sails across easily and quickly. She is pleased with her time, but she wasn't particularly challenged by the effort. The second rower has to cross on a very stormy day. The wind is blowing against her and the waves are huge. It is a long and exhausting battle, but she finally makes it across.

The first rower feels great about her abilities but may not be ready for stormy days. The second one wishes she'd done better, but she has learned that she is capable of getting through rough water.

Each time we struggle with something difficult, we gain a little skill and a little confidence about our ability to take on challenges. We get better at bouncing back, at surfing the waves that life occasionally sends us, whether they be little ripples or giant swells.

In her book *Adulting,* about what twenty-somethings need to know as they grow into responsible adults, Kelly Williams Brown (2013), herself a young adult, talks about life's unexpected challenges: "Sometimes these unexpected things will be small, short-term pains in the ass, like your car breaking down on the freeway when you are en route to a friend's wedding, or spilling coffee on your shirt before a job interview. Sometimes they will be enormous, long-term sorrows, like ongoing illness or the death of someone you love. But no matter what it is, you can handle it ... or, at least, act adult in the face of it" (218). Brown's assertion that you can handle anything that comes your way is an expression of confidence in your resilience.

Science Note: Mark Seery and his colleagues found evidence that "in moderation, whatever does not kill us may indeed make us stronger" (Seery, Homan, and Silver 2010). They looked at the effect of adversity on well-being and life satisfaction. You might guess that those with the least struggle fared best, but that wasn't true. Although high levels of stress were not good for anyone, moderate amounts of adversity (six to twelve lifetime negative events such as loss of a loved one, illness, or exposure to violence) actually produced the best outcomes. Compared to those with little to no adversity, the folks with moderate amounts of stress had the least distress and impairment and the most lifetime satisfaction. Obviously, severe levels of trauma are not good for anybody, particularly young children, but surviving moderate amounts of adversity can be beneficial. So next time you feel pushed around by life, be patient with yourself and remember that you will be even more resilient in the future.

CONTEMPLATE THIS:

You will not grow if you sit in a beautiful flower garden, but you will grow if you are sick, if you are in pain, if you experience losses, and if you do not put your head in the sand, but take the pain and learn to accept it, not as a curse or punishment but as a gift to you with a very, very specific purpose.

—Elisabeth Kübler-Ross

Meditation Builds Resilience

Luckily for us, meditation is challenging in just the right ways and is thus a great tool for building resilience. It is challenging partly because of how tricky it is to catch your mind when it veers out of the present and floats downstream. You build patience, focus, and the ability to persist each time your observing mind pulls you out of the river, back onto the bank, watching with compassionate acceptance the play of your thinking mind.

Meditation is also challenging because when you sit and watch your river of thought, you often discover some pretty uncomfortable stuff floating by. It is hard to sit with the inevitable, uncomfortable feelings that come along such as boredom, anger, sadness, or anxiety. With practice, though, your observing mind will grow in power, and you will find it gets easier to fully experience emotions without reacting *to* the emotions.

You start to see that thoughts and emotions come, but they also go. They don't have to define you or control you. You see that worrisome or painful thoughts and feelings are not the only occupants of your river. You recognize that there are also pleasant feelings as well as humorous and mundane thoughts. This complete view of the moment, one that holds all that is present—good, bad, and neutral—is a wide-angle view that is more balanced and thus more supportive of resilience, helping you stay afloat when the waves get rough.

Avoiding Avoidance

Because it is so easy to distract yourself from discomfort these days, you can begin to believe that it's possible to live a life free of unpleasant emotions. Our devices are always at hand to help us avoid many of life's annoyances. If you are standing in line and feel a bit of boredom, or at a party feeling shy, checking your phone buffers the discomfort.

Alcohol, drugs, and sex are all excellent sources of avoidance. Feeling unsatisfied or unhappy? Get high or drunk. Feeling lonely?

Hook up with a stranger on Tinder for some quick sex.

The downside of all this avoidance? If you are always avoiding the little headaches, then you will be vastly unprepared for the massive heartaches.

Discomfort Is Your Friend

Confronting the headaches and heartaches that come up in meditation will help you get better at managing the headaches and heartaches that surface during the rest of your life. Every time you sit calmly, breathing slowly, staying unperturbed by angry or self-critical thoughts floating by, you are building your willingness and capacity to tolerate discomfort. Increasing your capacity to tolerate discomfort is the key to developing resilience.

The converse of this is also true; if you regularly avoid every uncomfortable sensation, your capacity to tolerate discomfort steadily declines. In fact, there is some speculation that today's twenty-somethings lack resilience because their well-meaning parents have protected them from failure and disappointment to an unhelpful degree.

You can think of your capacity to tolerate discomfort as a magical bowl for holding your feelings that can shrink or expand, depending on your level of resilience. If you are not practiced at tolerating discomfort, your magical bowl shrinks down to the size of an espresso cup. One bad grade or a criticism from your boss, and your emotions are flooding over; you are overwhelmed and on the edge of not coping. However, if you practice tolerating discomfort—unpleasant sensations, thoughts, and feelings—during meditation, your cup will slowly expand and grow. Before long you'll have a giant latte bowl in front of you that can hold all manner of emotional distress without overflowing. You could have a fight with your boyfriend, miss the bus, and be late for work without feeling overwhelmed. That's strong resilience. That's surfing the waves with style.

Practice Tip: If you feel the urge to wiggle or scratch while meditating, use it as an opportunity to get familiar with and used to discomfort. Before you move, take three slow breaths, observing carefully where in your body you feel the desire to move and what happens to the urge if you just watch it without moving. You may find that it changes or even subsides if you stay curious about it without giving in to it.

It's All Temporary

Change is the only constant in life, so sayeth Heraclitus. Though he is long dead, his words remain true. You can be certain that however you are feeling right now, you will feel different soon. What is happening now will be over, and then something else will happen.

Nothing stays the same. Nothing. Some things last longer than others, but everything is impermanent. Everything. Even this beautiful planet on which we circle the sun. Even the sun we are circling.

Awareness of the temporary nature of your experience allows you to be patient when you are in a difficult patch. It is also what reminds you to give your full attention to those moments that are uplifting. Not taking pleasure and peace of mind for granted is what will allow you to recognize all the little delights in your day: a conversation with a good friend, laughing out loud, your favorite food, birdsong.

Not long ago I ran into Jamar, a student who had taken Koru a few months earlier. He told me that he was still meditating regularly and that his meditation practice had helped him discover that he was "capable of getting over anything." He told me, "When I was in high school, some bad stuff happened to me, stuff I thought would ruin my life. At some point, those things sort of faded into the background and I see now that they don't define my life anymore."

Jamar said that his meditation practice had helped him understand that even the most painful loss is temporary and that he could recover. Now, every time he feels disappointed or overwhelmed, he reminds himself, *This is temporary; I can get over anything,* and it helps him feel confident about his own resilience.

Equanimity: Peace of Mind in the Face of Adversity

Remember Maxine in the last chapter, who managed to feel "relatively calm" after she accepted she would have to rewrite her project when her computer crashed? That relatively calm state is what we call *equanimity.* Equanimity is a little hard to capture with words, but you will know it when you feel it. It is a state of open, balanced peace of mind that is cultivated by the practice of mindfulness.

Hip-hop mogul Russell Simmons (2014), who is a devoted meditator, defines equanimity as "evenness of mind, especially under stress," and says that he always thinks of it as just being "cool," sort of unflappable no matter what happens. Simmons says, "Whether the emotion is a happy or sad one, in order to achieve a state of equanimity, you need to stay focused on not getting stuck on it" (131). He's emphasizing that equanimity is not about suppressing feelings or reactions but rather experiencing them and letting them move on through.

You develop equanimity when you cease to sweat the small stuff because you see the big picture. It's like backing way up, getting an astronaut's view on your world. Rather than seeing the one storm cloud over your head, you see the whole, beautiful expanse of the sky. You see that across the full arc of your life, there will be stormy days and blue skies and everything in between. It's not that you don't prefer blue skies. You probably do. But you also understand that you can't control the weather, so you stay open to whatever the day brings, enjoying as best you can the sunny moments and the rainy ones, too.

Dealing with the Most Difficult Emotions

Tam said, "Meditating doesn't work for me. I mean, I feel a lot calmer while I'm meditating, but a few minutes after I stop, I start getting anxious again. The calmness doesn't last." I hear this a lot from new meditators who are trying to make some headway managing intense anxiety, worry, sadness, or anger. Understandably, it often leads them to give up, feeling that meditation won't help them find any lasting relief. If you are having this experience, there are a couple of things that might be helpful to know.

First, even if you only feel relief from your pain during the few minutes you are meditating, that is still a worthwhile exercise. During those few minutes, you are giving your nervous system a break from unrelenting tension and overstimulation. Even small breaks can be helpful as you train your nervous system to be less reactive and more resilient.

Second, as you accumulate minutes and hours of total time spent meditating, the benefits of the practice will start to spread beyond your meditation session. Once you put in enough time working with your discomfort during meditation, you will discover that you are able to access equanimity more often, even when you are not meditating.

I don't have any hard scientific data on how long this takes, and of course everyone is different. But in my experience, once you've logged ten to twenty hours of meditation, you will probably notice that some of your most difficult emotions get easier to manage. That may sound like a long time, but if you practice for thirty minutes twice a day, you might notice greater peace of mind in less than two weeks. It's challenging to devote that much time to meditation, but lots of people do. If you are serious about wanting to get relief from difficult emotions, it might be worth your time to give it a try. Consider using the gatha meditation we covered in chapter 8 when trying to stabilize your mind during rough emotional weather.

I don't want to suggest that all emotional challenges can be managed by meditation. Even the most experienced meditators can find themselves in situations that overwhelm them; at those times, consulting a counselor, doctor, or spiritual advisor is often the wisest course of action. However, even in those situations, making contact with the peacefulness that resides in the present moment can be calming.

Equanimity Fosters Resilience

Moments of equanimity will start to emerge during your meditation practice, and eventually they will start showing up in the rest of your life as well. You'll start to trust that whatever happens, you will be okay. You'll feel the pleasure of joyful moments without losing your head, and you'll feel the disappointment of losses without falling apart.

No matter what life brings you, you have options of how to respond. Building resilience by practicing meditation, learning acceptance, and developing equanimity are possible for all of us.

Hang in there and keep practicing; ten more minutes today will get you ready for some serious surfing.

Part 4

Developing Insight

Chapter 13

Mindfulness for Training Your Attention

By now, you are probably two to three weeks into your personal experiment with mindfulness. With any luck, your practice has given you real-life experience of the concepts we've covered so far, such as distinguishing between observing mind and thinking mind and using acceptance to move through difficulties. As we continue this journey, it's now time to learn a couple more skills.

First, I'll teach you guided imagery, a technique that is a bit different from the other skills in this book. Rather than focusing on your actual present-moment experience, you use your mind to create a different "place" to inhabit for a while. It's useful when you need a break from stress, insomnia, or physical pain.

The second skill in this chapter is a traditional mindfulness meditation technique called labeling. Like the gatha we learned in chapter 8, it is useful when your river of thought is running with Class V rapids.

Creating a Special Place

Imagery is a valuable tool for managing challenges (think intense worry or insomnia) or rehearsing for a performance (think hitting free throws or playing a violin concerto). When you engage all your senses to imagine a place or experience, your brain as well as the rest of your nervous system acts as if the experience is real. Imagined rehearsal can be as effective as actual rehearsal, and an imagined relaxing space can be as calming as an actual relaxing space. Thus, learning to use your mind to create a brief respite in your day is an effective stress management strategy.

With the imagery exercise we are going to practice, you will create in your mind's eye a place you can "visit" when you need to de-stress. Sometimes during this exercise my students will call to mind their childhood home or some other place they miss, and they experience feeling sad or homesick. If this happens to you, be aware it is a very normal experience. It is natural for imagery to evoke emotions associated with the places we imagine.

Many people find it soothing and comforting to "visit" a familiar spot, but others, particularly those with a history of trauma, have a better experience if they use a completely imaginary place, unrelated to any real-life experience. Do whatever works best for you. If it is too uncomfortable to visit a place from your past, then create an imaginary place, maybe something you've seen in pictures or read about in stories. If extremely painful emotions do arise, just open your eyes and end the exercise.

Guided Imagery

As the name suggests, this exercise really works best if it is guided, so I highly recommend you start out with the free recorded version of the exercise available on the Koru Mindfulness website, http://www.korumindfulness.org/guided-meditations. If you'd prefer to try it without the recording, read the following instructions through and then give it a try. It's best to do this exercise somewhere comfortable, either seated or lying down. Imagery is most effective when you bring all your senses to the imagined scene, noting how it feels, smells, sounds, and tastes as well as what you see with color and detail, so try to open up to all your senses as you progress through this exercise.

Instructions for Guided Imagery

Once you are seated somewhere comfortable, close your eyes. Call to mind a place in which you feel completely safe and comfortable. It can be a real place, somewhere you have been, either inside or outside. Or it can be an imaginary place. The only thing that matters is that it is a place you feel comfortable and safe. If more than one place comes to mind, just pick one and settle your attention on it.

Begin to visualize your special place in careful detail. Notice the colors and shapes around you. What is the temperature? Are you warm or cool? What are you wearing? Notice the sounds. Notice any fragrances. Feel your body resting in the space. Is there anything you can touch and feel in the space? Notice the qualities of the space that make it safe and comfortable.

Look around. Is there anyone or anything that you would like to add or take away to make the space even more comfortable and safe?

When your space is fully visualized, spend as long as you like soaking up the ambience, relaxing completely into the comfort and safety of the space you have created.

When you are ready to emerge, take your time. Become aware of the feel of your body, supported by whatever furniture you are resting on. Become aware of your breathing, watching a few slow, deep breaths. When you feel ready, open your eyes.

Special place imagery is a useful exercise any time your nervous system needs a break from stress. If you are having trouble falling asleep because your mind is spinning with too many thoughts, you can use imagery to quiet your mind. Getting a cavity filled? Perhaps you'd like to use imagery to construct a more comfortable space than the dentist's chair. If your work situation is particularly challenging, taking a midday break to "visit" a calming environment can be great stress relief.

Even though this exercise it not a pure mindfulness exercise, it does work well as an attention-training exercise and, as such, will support your mindfulness practice. Like all the skills you are learning, imagery takes practice. If you are a strong visual thinker, this skill will come more easily to you. If you don't tend to think in images, it may take longer to get the hang of it. Make sure you try it several times before forming an opinion about its usefulness to you.

Identifying and Releasing Thoughts

Labeling, sometimes called noting, is a commonly practiced meditation technique that builds on the work you have already done using observing mind to detect thoughts that pull you away during meditation. In this meditation, you will learn to identify or "label" thoughts as they appear in your mind.

Labeling helps you stay very alert to the presence of thoughts during your meditation. When thoughts appear, labeling them helps you observe them without getting pulled into their content so much, which makes it easier to release the thoughts and return to your breath, your anchor to the present moment.

Labeling takes advantage of the fact that our minds tend to produce certain types or patterns of thoughts. We've already talked about some common thought patterns such as judging your experience or wanting things to be different than they are. There are plenty of other thought patterns. For example, my mind is often busy making plans and lists of things to do. Other common thought patterns are worrying about the future or remembering events from the past.

When you label, you attach a descriptive word to your thoughts as soon as you notice them. The simplest way to begin is to say silently to yourself *thinking* any time you notice thoughts emerging. Some people like to use imagery with this exercise and will visualize an actual label. Some people say the descriptive word aloud to really anchor their attention. After you label the thought, you release it, returning your awareness to your breath as you stay alert for the next thought to come along.

If it becomes clear that particular types of thoughts are coming by, you can use more specific descriptive words. You can use "judging," "planning," "wanting," or any other word that fits the thought pattern you are seeing.

A common mishap with labeling is to get caught up in trying to decide on the exact "right" label. This of course is just more thinking. If you find yourself obsessing about which label to use, just go back to labeling it all "thinking."

Finally, be mindful of the tone of your "voice" when you label. Labels are observations, not criticisms. Try to label with kindness and curiosity *(Interesting. More judgments coming by)*, not impatience or disapproval *(WTF—I can't believe there are so many judgments).*

Enough thinking *about* labels. Lets give it a try.

Labeling Thoughts Meditation

You can use the free guided labeling thoughts meditation at http://www.korumindful ness.org/guided-meditations or read through the description below and practice on your own. You typically use labeling along with a breath awareness meditation. So to begin, set your meditation timer for at least ten minutes and get into your meditation position. See the Practice Tip in (see section entitled "Breath Awareness Meditation") if you need a reminder about your meditation posture.

Instructions for Labeling Thoughts Meditation

Depending on where you are seated, notice your feet and body making contact with the floor or chair. Notice your hands resting in your lap. Notice any sounds around you. Take a couple of deep, slow breaths, and then let your breathing be normal and natural, simple and easy. Without trying to change it in any way, begin to watch the rise and fall of your breath as it enters and leaves your body. Hold your awareness as best you can on the sensations of your breathing.

Stay alert for thoughts that bubble into your consciousness. When you recognize that your mind is thinking, say silently to yourself thinking *and then let the thoughts go as you return your awareness to your breath, your anchor to your present-moment experience.*

Each time thoughts appear, again label them "thinking" and come back to your breath. If it is clear that you are planning or judging or worrying, you can use those words for your labels. Don't fall into the trap of spending a lot of time thinking about your labels. Just notice the thoughts, label them, and return to the breath, letting your thoughts move away in the river of thought.

Remember, you are not trying to stop the thoughts. You will continue to have thoughts enter your mind, so you will continue to have the opportunity to notice, label, and release the thoughts. Let go of any judgments about whether you are doing it right or not. Just see those concerns as "judging" and then bring your awareness back to your breath.

Continue in this manner, cultivating curiosity, patience, and kindness until your meditation timer brings the session to a close. To end, take a deep breath, allow your eyes to open, and gently stretch your body in any way that feels comfortable.

Practice with labeling thoughts meditation until you feel you have the hang of it. By using labels, you become more familiar with the content of your river of thought. When you've practiced for a bit, see what patterns you're able to identify. Becoming aware of your most common thought patterns will bring you important insights about the way your mind works.

Practice Tip: Zen master Shunryu Suzuki (1970) said, "The most important point in our practice is to have right effort" (44). "Right effort" in meditation refers to the balanced effort you bring to your practice, staying present without any agenda other than to see what each moment brings.

When meditating, if you exert too much effort, especially if you try to achieve a particular mind state, you'll feel tense and frustrated, like you are putting a stranglehold on your mind. Before long, you'll dread your meditation time. If you apply no effort, then you are just relaxing, not meditating, and you are unlikely to see much progress, which ultimately will erode your motivation to keep at it.

To get an idea of right effort, think of a collegiate basketball player as she sets up for a free throw. If she uses too much force or effort, her shot will slam uselessly against the backboard. If she uses too little, then it's an air ball. To make the basket, it takes just the right touch. Similarly, effort that promotes a productive meditation practice is balanced: enough effort to keep yourself alert and open to whatever happens but not so much that you are generating frustration and self-criticism. Working with labels is a good way to cultivate right effort.

You can add these two new practices—guided imagery and labeling—to the collection of meditations and skills you can draw from for your daily ten minutes of mindfulness practice. Remember, the idea is that you will practice with all of the skills you've been learning so that you can discover which ones work best for you in any given situation. To get the most from your mindfulness practice, continue to record two things you are grateful for each day and do one of your everyday activities with full mindfulness.

It's time now to turn our attention to one of the most profound benefits of a regular mindfulness practice: increased self-understanding.

Chapter 14

Wisdom: Learning from Experience

Since you have made it this far, I'm going to let you in on a little secret. Though I've mostly been framing mindfulness as a way for you to cope with stress, in my mind the most profound power of mindfulness lies in self-discovery and the development of wisdom.

Wisdom is not the same as knowledge. Knowledge is the accumulation of information. You acquire knowledge when you study for an exam or learn a new programming language. Wisdom is insight into fundamental truths about yourself and your world. You have to experience life to acquire wisdom. You can know at what temperature water freezes and still not know what it feels like to be cold.

Wisdom develops as you observe the relationship between cause and effect in your life. You will have many opportunities to make these observations as you travel through your twenties. For example, you can acquire wisdom when you survive a bad breakup or experience the benefits of being kind to difficult colleagues. One student told me that he developed wisdom after he was forced to leave school for "partying instead of studying." Mindfulness facilitates this process by providing you with a tool for making nonjudgmental appraisals of all your experiences.

Don't Fail to Fail

Our best learning opportunities occur when we make mistakes or flat-out fail. We learn from our painful experiences if we are willing to be aware, nonjudgmentally, of the consequences of our choices and actions. Henepola Gunaratana (2001), a very wise teacher, says it this way: "Feeling the impact of your mistakes gives you great incentive to avoid them in the future" (162).

There's an old story that illustrates this truth:

Young Student: Wise teacher, what is the secret to happiness?

Wise Teacher: Good choices.

Young Student: How do I learn to make good choices?

Wise Teacher: Wisdom.

Young Student: How do I develop wisdom?

Wise Teacher: Bad choices.

The wise teacher knows that we learn when we recognize we have gone wrong and figure out how to do it differently next time. He also knows that wisdom is essential to creating a life that feels happy and satisfying. When we fear making mistakes so much that we are paralyzed and don't even try—either socially, academically or professionally—we rob ourselves of the opportunity to develop wisdom.

Nonjudgmental awareness illuminates both the choices that work out well and the ones that don't. For your mistakes to lead to greater wisdom, you have to resist the temptation to play the blame game (*It's your fault this happened*) or get mired in self-reproach (*I am so stupid. I never learn*) when you see you've screwed up. Instead, you observe what didn't work, and then do your best to make different choices next time. Keep in mind that you are not a bad person because you messed up; you just made a mistake. Learn from it and move on.

Science Note: Jeffrey Arnett, the psychologist who originally defined emerging adulthood as a distinct developmental stage, conducted surveys of his students at the

University of Maryland to better understand their attitudes on a number of topics. He found that the students' satisfaction with their college experience was primarily determined by their experiences of *personal growth.* Regardless of their academic experience, students deemed their college years successful if they perceived themselves to have matured through the process (Arnett 2004). This interest in personal growth—or, as I call it, the development of wisdom—is why twenty-somethings have so much to gain from mindfulness.

Seeing Causes and Consequences

Lakshmi was a senior struggling with decisions about her life after college. The closer she got to graduation, the more she partied, getting drunk most nights. She started a mindfulness practice and gradually became aware that her drinking was producing some negative consequences for her, especially when she'd do things while drunk that she regretted once she sobered up. She also could see that she was using her partying to avoid dealing with career decisions. One day Lakshmi said, "I've quit drinking for now. It wasn't what I'd planned for my last semester at Duke, but it feels like what I want to do. I don't want to judge anyone else, but for me, if I'm making choices when I'm drunk that I wouldn't otherwise make, I'm just putting up barriers between me and where I ultimately want to go."

Lakshmi began to actually *feel* different about her choices when her mindfulness practice opened her awareness to their consequences. It was this felt experience that motivated her to do things differently. This is what we mean when we say that wisdom—clear self-understanding—is "acquired experientially."

CONTEMPLATE THIS:

Yesterday I was clever, so I wanted to change the world. Today I am wise, so I am changing myself.

—Rumi

Diving Down into Authenticity

Mistakes are not the only route to the acquisition of wisdom, of course. By consistently developing nonjudgmental awareness and practicing mindfulness meditation, you open yourself up to endless opportunities for experiential learning.

Your conscious mind is like a vast ocean. The surface is choppy, influenced by the changing winds of your everyday life. The depths, though usually obscured by all the surface activity, are still and clear. By exploring these depths in meditation, you begin to discover your authentic values, desires, and beliefs.

When you are bobbing around on the surface of the ocean, you are pulled to and fro by the currents created by the opinions of your friends, your family, and the media. The desire for approval and the wish to avoid disappointing others, common to all of us, pull strongly on your perceptions. Though all of these factors are important reference points, none of them reveals your own personal truths. As your mindfulness develops, you will be able to drop into your mind's clear, still waters and discover what lies there. It's in this place of peaceful clarity that your most important insights arise.

Practice Tip: Try extending your meditation time at least once this week. Longer meditations will open opportunities for the choppy quality of your mind to settle so that you can more readily explore the clear depths, accessing deeper insights. Set your timer for twenty minutes. Use the technique of labeling your thoughts that we covered in chapter 13 to help you manage fear or restlessness that might bubble up when you tackle a longer sit; you can label it as "resistance" and then come back to your breath. Remember, long stretches of time are made up of moments that can be observed simply and easily, one breath at a time.

The Power of Awareness

Sometimes insights from meditation are life changing. One day Dominic announced in his Koru class, "I decided I'm not going to law school." Dominic told us that though law school had been his goal for years, his mindfulness practice had helped him discover that "I actually have zero interest in the stuff that lawyers do. I can't tell you how good it feels to realize this; it's like I've just been reprieved from a prison sentence!"

When Dominic was able to observe and accept his true feelings about becoming a lawyer, it was abundantly clear to him that law school was not for him. He could see his authentic feelings once he got underneath his reactions to what he believed others wanted or admired. The new information gave him the confidence to change course.

I want to be clear that I am not saying that everybody will change their life path once they start meditating. Mindfulness certainly doesn't cause us all to abandon our plans. We are all different. Some of us want to go to law school.

Most of us don't. It's just good to know the best choices for you personally, and mindfulness can help you figure it out.

CONTEMPLATE THIS:

Mindfulness is like turning on a light in an attic. Light shows the treasures, old junk we thought we'd gotten rid of, dusty corners that need clearing out. But it doesn't matter how long the attic has been dark or how much stuff is there, you can still switch on the light and take a look.

—Sharon Salzberg

Little Insights Add Up

Sometimes our wisdom derives less from great insights and more from the little truths that bob into our awareness as our mindfulness practice develops. I have long lists of insights students in my Koru classes have shared over the years. For example, one student was surprised to see how quickly his mind tried to find someone to blame if something didn't go his way; he recognized that this reflex was his way of protecting himself from worries about his own culpability. He said, "I realize now that not everything has to be someone's fault."

Another student observed the way her constant comparisons to other students fed her feelings of inadequacy and kept her from appreciating her own strengths. Someone else realized that almost all of her choices about how she spent her time were based on feelings of guilt about what she "should" be doing. She saw how this created chronic resentment in her that was not healthy for her or her relationships.

Yet another student reported that he was getting familiar with the relationship between his energy levels, ability to concentrate, and efficiency at completing his work. This allowed him to make adjustments to his study schedule that increased his productivity and decreased his sense of stress.

These little insights pile up, adding to our self-understanding, helping us make little adjustments in our behaviors that over time can put us on the course to living more satisfying and meaningful lives.

Authentic Does Not Mean Permanent

Whether by the accumulation of little lessons or the uncovering of life-changing insights, mindfulness promotes self-understanding. However, it is important to understand that you don't actually have a solid, unchanging, authentic self that will be revealed if you meditate long enough. Instead, as your observations of your mind become more fine-tuned, you will discover an internal landscape composed of an assortment of changing—often conflicting—feelings, attitudes, and energies. What is present and expressed is the product of the circumstances of the moment. For example, you will respond differently to a friend in need if you are returning home sleep-deprived after a difficult exam than you will if you are well rested and feeling pleased by some recent accomplishment. Thus, at different times and in different contexts you will feel and behave differently. Mindfulness allows you to be aware of the factors influencing you in the moment and creates the opportunity to make wise choices about what feelings and attitudes you wish to cultivate and express.

These in-the-moment choices are strongly influenced by your perceptions about what really matters in life, a topic we'll explore in the next chapter.

Chapter 15

Values: What Matters?

"The reality that people often wake up to is that life is a gift they have been taking for granted, and that people matter more than money" (Haidt 2006, 140). According to Jonathan Haidt, author of *The Happiness Hypothesis,* this is the insight that people often arrive at after being diagnosed with a potentially terminal illness. This sudden clear awareness inspires them to live differently during the time they have left. And their regrets? Do they regret they didn't make more money or work harder? Nope. They regret they did not understand sooner the intrinsic value in each moment of their lives.

It's tragic, really, waiting until you are facing death to recognize what is valuable in life. Learning you have little time left pulls you hard into the present, exposing clearly what is most important. Fortunately, contemplative practices like meditation do the same thing. Thus, you can begin right now to grasp that your life is both time limited and precious.

Achieving Instead of Being

In our culture we prize doing and achieving over just being. Now, achievement is a good thing. You could justly label me a hypocrite if I said otherwise. But, there is more to life than achievement. That end-of-life insight into the value of life affirms this. There is so much joy and wisdom in just being. There are ignored miracles in every moment. Think about this one: with every breath you pull air into your body, extract the oxygen from it to power your cells, and then return the air back to the environment. Now, that's impressive. Surely it's up there with any other achievement you could possibly dream up.

CONTEMPLATE THIS:

People travel to wonder at the height of mountains, at the huge waves of the sea, at the long courses of rivers, at the vast compass of the ocean, at the circular motion of the stars; and they pass themselves by without wondering.

—Saint Augustine

Being Instead of Achieving

Remember this distinction from chapter 10: You are not a human doing. You are a human being. Your life has value because you exist, no matter how long your list of achievements. Life is absolutely remarkable, but because our day-to-day happenings are so commonplace, we experience it as mundane. Think about it. You grew from a small seed inside your mother's womb. You developed into a being whose consciousness is so complex and mysterious that it defies explanation by even the most advanced neuroscientists. Somehow your 100 billion neurons link together in a way that produces self-awareness. Unlike any other animal, you can think about thinking. Getting in touch with the magic of your life force can shake you awake so you stop taking it all for granted.

Discovering Your Values

If you want to deemphasize achieving and emphasize being, you have to change the questions you organize your life around. Instead of asking, *What do I want to accomplish?* ask, *Starting now, what do I want my life to be about? What kind of person do I want to be?*

The answers to these questions direct you to a present-focused life, organized around that which has meaning. When you start considering what you want your life to be about, qualities like forming solid relationships, making a difference, and having financial security will likely come to mind. These are values that can be acted on in any moment; you don't have to wait to achieve anything in particular to actualize what you care about.

Your values are a mash-up of the values you learned from your family, your friends, various mentors, and the media. They evolve as you age, because your life experience has a powerful impact on your values. Taking a class on economics or environmental science, struggling to pay your bills while you work a low-wage job, witnessing or experiencing oppression and injustice, or losing a loved one in adolescence or early adulthood—these kinds of experiences and innumerable others shape your identity and your sense of what matters.

Like a compass that points you in the direction you wish to head, your values can inform all the turns you take in your life. But you have to look at the compass to benefit from it, and the compass resides inside you, underneath the choppy surface of your thinking mind.

CONTEMPLATE THIS:

Most people think of success as achieving goals. I invite clients to consider a different definition: success is living by our values. With this definition, we can be successful right now even though our goals may be a long way off (and even though we may actually never achieve them).

—Russ Harris

TAKE A MOMENT: You can learn more about your values by taking the free Life Values Inventory (LVI) at http://www.lifevalu esinventory.org. The LVI helps you identify-your values and shows you how to use the information to direct important life decisions.

Alternatively, make a list of the things you care most about. You might consider listing financial security, concern for others, concern for the environment, independence, spirituality, creativity, health and fitness, personal pleasure, and family and friends. If you think of others, include them, too. Now rank these things in order of what you care most about. Then rank them again, this time in order of what you spend the most time on. Do the two lists match up, or are the things you care most about what you spend the least time on? Think about how you could adjust your life to get the two lists more in sync. The narrower the gap between your behaviors and your values, the happier you will be.

Practice Tip: You can orient your mind in the direction of present-moment awareness by setting a clear intention before you begin your meditation session. Before you start your timer, call to mind your intention to nonjudgmentally hold your awareness in the moment. Let go of any specific goals for the meditation *(I hope I feel relaxed when this is over),* and instead be open to watching each breath as best you can, being willing to simply see what happens.

You Have What You Need

Emphasizing *being* over *achieving* leads to the understanding that in this moment you likely have absolutely everything you need to be happy. The Antarctic explorer Admiral Richard E. Byrd (Byrd [1938] 2003), having spent much time facing severe hardship, concluded that "half the confusion in the world comes from not knowing how little we need" (57). When you are anchored in the present, your confusion about this diminishes.

I was sitting in a café once and overheard a conversation between a dad and his son, who looked to be about three years old. The dad was trying to teach his son about the difference between "wants" and "needs." Pointing to his son's sneakers where a small toe was visible poking through a large hole, the dad said, "Looks like it is time for new shoes for you. Do you *need* new shoes or do you *want* new shoes?" The boy stared at his shoes for a moment, and then looking up said, "These are good shoes. I'm keeping these shoes."

The boy was teaching his dad an even more important lesson: how to be happy with what you have. Kids get this. They know that value is not tied to the appearance of perfection. They know how to get intense pleasure out of what's in front of them, instead of always looking for something better. As we grow up, we cease to recognize the perfection in front of us, unable to see through its disguise as a worn-out pair of shoes.

Ethical Behavior

It is easier to feel the perfection in each moment if you have the peace of mind that comes from making ethical choices. Your ethics—your beliefs about what opinions and behaviors are right and wrong—are strongly influenced by your values. We usually talk of ethics in terms of moral prescripts that are set up by a society or religion, but here I'm talking about your own *personal* ethics.

Generally meditation teachers steer away from words like "right" and "wrong" because they are so judgy; we prefer instead to use the words "skillful" and "unskillful." In this context, skillful means choices that are consistent with your personal ethics and lead to peace of mind. Unskillful decisions feel uncomfortable to you in some way—agitating the mind, keeping you awake at night, or leading to other forms of discomfort like unhealthy levels of shame or guilt.

If you personally believe that it is wrong to cheat on your boyfriend, and you do it anyway, you have violated your own ethics and you are probably going to feel bad about it. Thus, I would say that the choice to cheat was unskillful, and the consequence will be lack of peace of mind. You set yourself up for lots of unnecessary misery if you make unskillful choices over and over again.

A regular meditation practice leads to more ethical behavior simply because it casts the light of precise, nonjudgmental awareness on your choices and their consequences. You notice when your behavior is skillful (promotes peace of mind) and when it's not (disrupts peace of mind).

Greater peace of mind means less suffering. All humans want to suffer less. As you become more aware of the causes of suffering for yourself and others, you will inevitably shift your behavior in the direction of less suffering. Unless you are a psychopath (and you probably aren't, statistically speaking), you won't be able to help yourself.

TAKE A MOMENT: Sit comfortably, eyes closed, and drop your awareness into your body. Feel your body breathing in and out. Call to mind a time when you did or said something that you regretted or worried about afterward. Notice, was the regret or worry the result of behavior that conflicted with your personal ethics? Next time you are in a similar situation, and you are fully aware, could you make a different choice that would lead to greater peace of mind?

CONTEMPLATE THIS:

Do the best you can until you know better. Then when you know better, do better.
—Maya Angelou

Rigid Dogmatism Is No Fun

Being overly attached to your personal ethics can be as problematic as being clueless about them. Overattachment to views and values leads to rigid dogmatism. Rigid dogmatism is no fun. Worse, rigid dogmatism keeps you from learning and evolving. In fact, if you are very attached to a particular viewpoint, and you are given information that refutes it, you are likely to believe your original view even more strongly (Nyhan and Reifler 2010). So that's a problem. Obviously, the inability to consider and incorporate new information interferes with growth and change. If you can be aware of your values and ethics but hold them a bit lightly, you can be open-minded, interested in learning from others who see the world differently.

Your mindfulness skills will alert you when you are clinging too tightly to your views. The telltale sign is often a surge of agitation or anger when confronted with a different point of view. When you feel that surge, take a deep breath and pause before saying or doing anything. Remember that there are many different perspectives—all informed by different values and life experiences. Try to let go of the desire to be "right" or the impulse to see the other as "wrong," a natural but typically unhelpful reflex. We all want the same thing in the end—to be free from suffering; we just have different ideas about how to get there.

Blissed Out

Being guided by your values and personal ethics is not the same as following your bliss. Young adults are often advised to follow their bliss by making career choices they feel passionate about. To my mind this advice is perhaps not as helpful as it might seem.

For one thing, not everybody has a passion that translates into a job. I often see students paralyzed by their inability to identify a passion that lends itself to reliable employment. More importantly, most of the jobs out there that need doing are not the kinds of jobs people feel great passion for. Many of these jobs are the ones that twenty-somethings do to make ends meet: waiting tables, washing dishes, landscaping, and child care. Overemphasizing the importance of passion-driven pursuits ignores the satisfaction that comes from doing any kind of work with attention to the quality and value of the work.

The advice to follow your bliss overlooks the truth that your bliss is right here, right now. Don't follow it into the future; follow it into the present. Awakening in the morning in a warm bed is blissful. Sating your hunger or quenching your thirst is blissful. Being smiled at by a stranger is blissful. Bliss is nothing special in that it is not rare; it is here, all the time. At the same time, because it can be so hard to see, it is the most precious treasure in the world.

CONTEMPLATE THIS:

You wander from room to room
Hunting for the diamond necklace
That is already around your neck!

—Rumi

No one can tell you what matters and expect it to make an impact. This is a piece of wisdom you have to experience to feel its relevance. Short of being diagnosed with a terminal illness, your meditation practice is the surest path to the discovery of the riches available in all the moments of your life.

Chapter 16

The Skill of Happiness

Rather than simply luck of the draw, happiness is a skill that can be learned. That's the position of Matthieu Ricard, a French scientist and Buddhist monk who has studied the topic extensively. Ricard (2006) defines happiness as "a deep sense of flourishing that arises from an exceptionally healthy mind. This is not a mere pleasurable feeling, a fleeting emotion, or a mood, but an optimal state of being" (19).

Our happiness in life is primarily shaped by three factors. First, our genetically determined temperament accounts for roughly half of our level of happiness. That's the part we can't do much about.

Next, the circumstances of our lives are responsible for a surprisingly small fraction of our happiness—only about 10 percent. This explains why you can find unhappy people who seem to have everything and very happy people who have suffered much hardship. The actual circumstances of your life don't count for much.

Finally, the remaining 40 percent is determined by our intentional behaviors, a reflection of how we think about and relate to the circumstances of our lives (Lyubomirsky, Sheldon, and Schkade 2005). Thus, if you consider just the factors important to happiness that are mutable—your life circumstances and the way you think about and relate to your circumstances—the thinking and relating part is responsible for 80 percent of your happiness. It's that hefty portion that Ricard is referring to when he says that happiness is an acquired skill.

Practicing Happiness

If happiness is a skill, then like all skills it takes practice. How do you practice happiness? You guessed it: meditation.

Ricard was one of the experienced meditators studied by researchers looking at the long-term effects of meditation. Pico Iyer (2014) said about their findings that after testing many subjects "who had meditated for ten thousand hours or more and many who had not, [the researchers] felt obliged to conclude that those who had sat still for years had achieved a level of happiness that was, quite literally, off the charts, unseen before in the neurological literature" (25).

Ten thousand hours is a lot of meditating, so if you want off-the-charts happiness, you had best get started. Fortunately, most of us will settle for on-the-charts happiness, which doesn't take nearly as many hours of practice to achieve. I hadn't been meditating for long before I recognized that I was more lighthearted, and I've heard a similar report from many of my Koru students.

Happiness vs. Pleasure

Happiness can be confused with pleasure, though actually they are quite distinct. Pleasure is fleeting, but happiness is enduring. Pleasure depends on circumstances outside of ourselves, while happiness depends on our internal conditions, mainly our state of mind. You can feel pleasure at someone else's expense, but not happiness. It doesn't work that way.

Think of something that gives you pleasure: a hot shower, a delicious meal, acquiring a pair of fancy shoes, or even great sex. All of those things are briefly wonderful, but they end, or at least the pleasure they bring does. If they went on interminably, they'd cease to be pleasurable; you're going to want to get out of that shower eventually.

Real happiness is an enduring state of sublime peace of mind that you never tire of, but you do have to ceaselessly cultivate.

Cultivating Happiness

Cultivating happiness takes thoughtfulness and care, just like cultivating a lush garden. Your mindfulness meditation practice is an essential ingredient. It prepares and nourishes the soil, keeping it healthy. Your mindfulness practice also offers up the insights about your values and views that direct your choice of seeds to plant. Generally the seeds of happiness are positive mind states, such as gratitude, generosity, kindness, humility, and compassion.

Some people worry that they could lose their competitive edge if they cultivate too much positivity. In his book *10% Happier,* ABC news anchor Dan Harris (2014) shares his struggle with this conundrum. As his meditation practice increased his compassion and kindness, he worried he was losing the cunning and aggressiveness he needed to succeed in the competitive world of TV news. He eventually learned he didn't have to jettison his ambition as he became less of a "jerk," and his career continued to advance alongside his meditation practice. He says, "Compassion has the strategic benefit of winning you allies. And then there's the small matter of the fact that it makes you a vastly more fulfilled person" (Harris 2014, 209).

Research on happiness supports the contention that positivity doesn't interfere with achieving life's important goals. Happiness has been shown to produce a long list of tangible benefits including higher odds of getting married, lower odds of divorce, more friends, stronger social support, greater creativity, increased productivity, and higher income (Lyubomirsky, Sheldon, and Schkade 2005).

All these findings mirror my personal observations. I've never seen anyone become less successful as a result of becoming a happier, nicer person. Unless your heart's desire is to become a vengeful autocrat, I doubt it will interfere with your goals.

Watch Out for the Weeds

For your garden to flourish, you have to stay on top of the weeds. The weeds are negative mind states, such as greed, jealousy, intolerance, and hatred. As your observing mind develops, you'll catch yourself being judgmental or rude, and you'll notice the discomfort this causes in others. You won't like the way it feels, and little by little you'll start doing it less. This is how you spot the weeds and move them out, creating room for the seeds you are planting to grow. Russell Simmons (2014) has experienced this process himself. He says, "When you move all that judgment out of your heart, it's not like that space sits there empty.

No, when you get rid of the judgment, what actually replaces it is compassion" (164).

Jason, one of my former Koru students, shared what he'd noticed about the way his emotional life had shifted over the course of four years of regular meditation practice. Early on he recognized some uncomfortable patterns, like getting cranky when people got in his way when he was biking to work, saying things that just "reinforced my ego," and not listening well to others. He said, "At first I didn't know what to do, because it seemed like the harder I tried to rectify these ways of thinking the more they seemed to persist. But eventually, I started to just breathe whenever I noticed them, which gave me a little extra space to react differently, or simply to let go and to be kind to myself in spite of these habits. And over time, some of these habits have begun to change." Now, he sees that he is much more attuned to how others are feeling and finds it much easier to forgive even the most difficult people. He's less likely to get irritated over minor matters, and he enjoys listening to others and hearing about their successes. Finally, he said about his meditation practice, "It's a difficult road, but it seems ultimately a road to peace, and I'm glad I was able to start on that road at the beginning of my PhD."

Jason's meditation practice taught him to be aware of thoughts and behaviors that he didn't particularly like without layering on unhelpful self-criticism. In the light of this nonjudgmental appraisal, his negativity began to abate. Jason is now happy with his life and thriving with his work, but he'll be the first to tell you it takes work to get there—and that it is worth it.

Science Note: Scientists at Northeastern University constructed a clever study to find out whether or not meditation actually leads to compassionate action (Condon et al. 2013). First, they taught half of their study subjects to meditate. Then, they sent all of the subjects to an appointment, where they had to wait to be seen. The waiting room was set up with three chairs, with two actors already seated when the subject arrived, forcing the subject to sit in the only remaining chair. A few minutes later, a third actor entered the room on crutches and in obvious pain. The two already-seated actors conspicuously ignored the suffering person. The test: would the subjects who had learned meditation respond compassionately more frequently than those who had not?

It turns out the meditators were much more likely to respond compassionately, proving to be over 300 percent more likely to give up their chairs than the non-meditators. Whether the meditators were more aware of the suffering or just felt more bothered by it is unclear.

Regardless, the meditators' behavior was significantly more compassionate.

One of the authors, David DeSteno, said about the study, "The truly surprising aspect of this finding is that meditation made people willing to act virtuous—to help another who was suffering—even in the face of a norm not to do so. The fact that the other actors were ignoring the pain creates a 'bystander-effect' that normally tends to reduce helping" (Northeastern University 2015).

Behaving Happy

Engaging in the behaviors that support positive mind states goes a long way toward cultivating happiness. Be aware that you can't force yourself to feel anything in particular, and there's no point judging yourself for not feeling the way you think you should. Quite simply, we feel what we feel, but we do get to choose our actions. We can choose to behave in ways that create the conditions for positive mind states to develop and thrive.

There are a number of behaviors that have been shown to promote happiness. For example, altruism—doing good things for other people without the expectation of personal gain—will make you happy. When compared to pleasurable activities, altruistic behavior creates a longer-lasting boost in mood (Haidt 2006).

Other behaviors that lead to happiness include developing gratitude and performing acts of generosity. No matter how you feel, you can engage in these behaviors. Rather than waiting to feel happy so you can behave happy, try behaving happy and see what happens.

CONTEMPLATE THIS:

Life's most persistent and urgent question is, "What are you doing for others?"
—Martin Luther King, Jr.

TAKE A MOMENT: Today, before you sleep, do—without any expectation of gain—one good deed for someone else. Tomorrow do the same. Notice how that behavior impacts your mood and your day. If it seems useful, you could make a commitment to doing an act of kindness daily.

As your mindfulness practice progresses, you are likely to find that you are less critical of yourself and others, quicker to help others, and less likely to say and do things that you regret. This may all result in your feeling happier as well. If you've been meditating daily as you've worked your way through this book, you may already be able to detect the early signs of these changes. I'm hoping that you are so intrigued by these developments that you will keep at it, continuing to cultivate your happiness garden ten minutes at a time.

Part 5

Carrying On

Chapter 17

Mindfulness for Enriching Your Life

Congratulations! You've made your way to the final two Koru skills. In this chapter you will learn about eating meditation and labeling feelings. Eating meditation is just like it sounds: using the myriad of sensations that accompany eating as your object of meditation. Eating meditation is often the first skill that you learn when you are introduced to mindfulness, but our Koru students have repeatedly said they thought it was best to save this mindfulness skill for the end. The experience you've acquired with mindfulness so far will make this meditation even more powerful.

Labeling feelings meditation expands on the labeling thoughts meditation you learned in chapter 13. Labeling practice in general is a slightly advanced skill, and labeling emotions takes some steadiness of mind, which is why it is the last meditation that we teach. It is particularly useful, as it offers a strategy for working with the sometimes-intense emotions that underlie our most repetitive thought patterns.

Eating: An Undervalued Pleasure

Eating is typically an underappreciated activity. Though eating is an opportunity to experience pleasure multiple times throughout the day, most of us barely notice our meals, mindlessly shoving our food down while we stare at our devices.

In our modern Western culture, most of us have an abundance of delicious foods available to us. In contrast to our poor ancestors, who had no choice during hard winter months to eat anything but dried out roots and nuts, we carefully select our food from plentiful and varied options, deciding what seems most satisfying in the moment. And then we gobble it down, paying almost no attention to the flavor extravaganza happening in our mouths.

Eating Meditation

Eating meditation is about changing that pattern. It's about opening your awareness fully to all that is miraculous about consuming delicious, life-giving food. Eating meditation honors the richness of the complete experience, from acknowledging the origins of the food to tasting every molecule of flavor on your tongue. Even simple foods become remarkable when held in full awareness.

Instructions for Eating Meditation

To do an eating meditation, find something simple to eat, like a piece of fruit. Grapes, berries, or a slice of apple are good choices. Find a quiet place to sit undisturbed. Place your food in your lap or on a table in front of you.

Close your eyes and take a couple deep, slow breaths. When you feel ready, open your eyes and gaze at the food in front of you. Notice the color, shape, and texture. Notice any feelings in your body or any thoughts you have as you look at the food. Reflect for a moment on the journey the food has taken to end up here. Somebody somewhere planted the seeds. The sun and rain fell upon the dirt; the plant grew. Somebody harvested it and transported it all the way to the store, where you purchased it. It's a minor miracle that you have in front of you a delicious morsel that sprouted from the soil.

Take the food into your hand and continue to stay curious about all you notice. What does it feel like? What is the texture, the temperature, the weight? Notice any thoughts you have as you look at the food. Are there any sensations in your mouth that might be signaling a wish to eat it?

Bring the food up to your nose, and see if you can detect any aroma. Place the food in your mouth and hold it there without chewing for a few moments.

What do you notice? Flavor? Texture? Temperature? A desire to begin chewing? Other thoughts? Once you have made careful observations, begin chewing, just one bite at a time. What happens when you bite into the food? What happens to the flavor? How do your mouth and tongue work? Where do you taste the flavor?

Continue to chew slowly without swallowing, noticing as much as you can about the experience. Pay attention to what your tongue does and how your teeth come together. Finally, when you are ready to swallow, pay careful attention to how that action occurs. What muscles are at work to move your food down your throat? At what point do you lose the ability to detect the food as you swallow?

What are the thoughts, feelings, and sensations you now notice, having swallowed a single bite of food?

Now begin again, with another bite of the same food. Carefully observing the appearance and aroma of the food, before beginning to taste and chew the food. Take several bites in *this manner, engaging entirely in the experience of eating.*

As with any other meditation, your mind will wander off at times. When you notice your mind has wandered, just bring it back again to the sensations associated with eating.

When you are finished, sit quietly with your eyes closed for a few minutes, watching your breath, noticing how your body feels. When you are ready, open your eyes and stretch in any way that feels comfortable for your body.

What did you notice about eating meditatively that was different from your usual experience of eating? Most people are pretty amazed by the complexity of the fragrance, tastes, and muscle movements involved in eating when they slow down and pay careful attention to the process.

There are a number of advantages to slowing down your eating. For one, when you eat mindfully, you extract as much pleasure as possible from the experience. Paying attention to the small, everyday pleasures in your life will help balance your awareness of the more difficult aspects of life.

Another advantage: slowing down your eating helps you eat more healthily, in both the quality and quantity of your food. We have all eaten beyond the point of comfortable fullness at times. Usually this happens because it takes a few minutes for your brain to register that your stomach is full. If you eat very quickly, you will stuff yourself past the full point before your brain has a chance to catch up. Slowing down gives your body a chance to recognize and communicate that you have had enough to eat.

After learning eating meditation, my students often say to me, "Wow. That was really slow. It would take forever to eat an entire meal like that." It actually wouldn't take forever. Forever is a long time. But it would take quite a while. You could try it if you like, just to see how it feels to enjoy a meal with complete awareness of the total experience.

Of course, you don't have to eat your whole meal mindfully to get the benefits of mindful eating. Even slowing down a little bit can make a difference. To slow yourself down so that you eat more mindfully, put your fork down between each bite. Something about this simple act pulls your attention more fully into the flavors in your mouth. Alternatively, try taking the first bite of every meal with full mindfulness or try drinking your morning coffee with this level of awareness. See if you notice any benefit from even a small change in the way you consume your food or drinks.

Labeling Your Feelings

In chapter 13 you learned how to use labels to work with your thoughts. Now you will learn to add your feelings to the content of your mind that you label. To review, you label your thoughts by noticing when thoughts (words or images) come into your mind, then silently noting to yourself, *thinking,* before you return your attention to your breath. If you notice that the content of the thoughts is mostly planning, judging, or worrying, you can use those words to describe your thoughts. Or you can pick any other word to use, so long as you don't get too entangled in thoughts about what label to use.

If you have been practicing labeling your thoughts, you have likely noticed that some thoughts go round and round. They keep coming back, sometimes with a great deal of discomfort and intensity, and you may start to feel frustrated, wishing you could stop them. Often these types of thoughts are fed by strong emotions.

Some people have emotions that are powerful, constant, and overwhelming. Others find it hard to detect and identify their emotions at all. Emotions are usually experienced as physical sensations in your body, such as a knot in the stomach, pressure in the chest, or tingling and warmth in your face or extremities. Your feelings generate thoughts, and often the thoughts, which are filled with content about the emotion, get confused with the emotion itself. For example, say your roommate leaves his stuff everywhere. This makes you feel mad at him, and your mind generates thoughts about what a jerk he is. The words or images—the thoughts—are about him being a jerk. The feelings are the sensations your nervous system creates in your body when you are reacting with anger.

Just as you can't get a pot to stop boiling by holding the lid on tightly, you can't get emotionally laden thoughts to stop bubbling by clamping down on them. You have to turn down the heat if you want a pot of water to stop boiling, and the same is true of a mind boiling from emotional heat. Bringing calm, cooling awareness to the emotion that is fueling the thought pattern will often slow the boiling. Becoming aware of and labeling the feeling, and watching it with curiosity, allows the heat to dissipate. When you turn your attention back to your breath, you aren't pushing the feeling down or away; you're just shifting your gaze. The feeling may call your attention again soon, but that's okay.

While you're meditating, any emotion might be present. If you detect an emotion, you can just label it "feeling," or if it is clear to you what you are feeling, you can label it more specifically: fear, anger, joy, sadness, regret, contentment. If you are unclear about what you are experiencing, just label it "confusion" and welcome it. As you continue to observe the workings of your mind like a scientist, you will learn to discern the differences between your various feeling states.

Labeling Feelings Meditation

You can follow these instructions for a labeling feelings meditation or you can find guided audio at http://www.korumindfulness.org/guided-meditations or in the Koru app.

Instructions for Labeling Feelings Meditation

To practice labeling feelings, get into your seated meditation position and set your timer for at least ten minutes. Begin just as you did with the labeling thoughts meditation, first finding your breath and letting your attention settle there. If you notice thoughts, instead of struggling with them or judging them, just label them and return your attention to your breath.

Are there thoughts that keep returning with an edgy intensity? If so, can you notice what is beneath them? Is there an emotion you can detect? Can you bring it into full awareness and notice where you feel it in your body? Often we can feel emotions as sensations in our stomach or chest. Notice the difference between the felt sensation of the emotion itself and the thoughts that are generated by the emotion.

As you hold the emotion in your awareness, label it "feeling." If the nature of the emotion is very clear to you, label it more precisely: "anger," "joy," "fear," "contentment," or whatever seems closest. Try to detect if you are either hanging onto the feeling or forcing it away. See if you can create enough space to accept, even welcome, the feeling without trying to change it.

Whatever you are feeling now, be it pleasant or unpleasant, is temporary. If you can allow your observing mind to hold it in awareness without reacting to it, you will be able to see the way the intensity shifts and changes. Emotions are very interesting, so you can watch them with the objectivity of a scientist until they fade or you are ready to turn your attention back to your breath.

Continue in this manner, cultivating curiosity and patience until your meditation timer brings the session to a close. To end, take a deep breath, allow your eyes to open, and gently stretch your body in any way that feels comfortable.

Learning to identify, name, and hold your feelings in awareness is a valuable skill to develop. Working with this meditation can help you change your relationship to your feelings so that you fear and avoid them less and are thus less controlled by them. Learning to recognize and work with your emotions is an important part of creating healthier relationships, a topic we'll cover in the next chapter. But first, take a moment to practice observing your emotions.

TAKE A MOMENT: It takes a very powerful mindfulness muscle to observe and accept the most intense emotions. It can be helpful to practice with more subtle emotions, learning to feel the emotion in your body and identify it, separating it out from the story that thinking mind tells about the emotion. Take a moment to explore your emotions. Sit with your eyes closed, notice your breath, and then drop your awareness into your body. Do you detect any sensations that signal an emotion? Maybe you notice a subtle emotion like boredom or contentment? Sometimes you actually notice the story first and then look underneath it to find the inciting emotion. Get as curious as you can about the physical sensations that tell you about the emotion. Practice watching the emotion with curiosity and compassion. Breathe slowly and deeply, opening up around the feeling, giving it plenty of space. Notice if it moves or changes. Try to neither invite it nor push it away. Accept it just as it is. Let any thoughts about the emotion move on down your river of thought. Take as long as you like with this exercise.

These last two meditations round out your collection of mindfulness practices, which now includes ten different meditations and skills. By now you may be developing your favorites, the ones that resonate most with you and that you find most useful. Take the time you need to practice these last two skills, and see if you can integrate them into your budding mindfulness practice.

Chapter 18

Relating Mindfully

There is probably no greater contributor to your happiness than the number and quality of your relationships with friends, family, lovers, and colleagues. Our relationships are important; humans *need* relationships. We have evolved to be dependent on our connections with others. Just as our ancestors were unlikely to prosper if they got kicked out of the cave, our happiness and success in life hinges in large part on our ability to form healthy attachments (Haidt 2006).

Whether you are forging new relationships or deepening existing connections, your mindfulness skills will be of service. In the chapter on happiness, we explored the way meditation helps bring forward your naturally benevolent qualities so that you become a bit kinder, more patient, and less selfish—changes that will improve your ability to play well with others. Other aspects of mindfulness, such as learning to be present so that you listen better, speak more thoughtfully, and manage your emotional reactions more carefully, will also enhance your connections. All of these factors add up to healthier, more satisfying relationships.

CONTEMPLATE THIS:

I've learned that people will forget what you said, people will forget what you did, but people will never forget how you made them feel.
—Maya Angelou

Mindful More; Mindless Less

Mindlessness is hard to say but easy to do. Many a relationship snafu has mindlessness at its core.

Mindlessness of Emotional Undercurrents

Mindlessness results in conflict when we are clueless about our internal emotional state. Uncomfortable emotions such as jealousy, anger, and resentment are all normal parts of human relationships. Like cyclones swirling down from the sky, destructive words or deeds are spawned by our stormy emotions. Ever picked a fight with someone after you had a bad day at school or work? Ever blamed your partner or a roommate for a problem that you created?

Ever lost a friend because you couldn't admit you were wrong?

We've all done things like this and more, often because we were simply unaware of the emotional processes at play inside of us. We all develop patterns of reaction that strongly influence our behaviors; if left unexamined they can have toxic effects on our relationships. Mindfulness helps you hold your emotional reactions and patterns in full awareness, which gives you the chance to decide how you want to behave in the moment.

For example, I have learned that when I am tired I feel irritable and my thinking mind starts generating criticisms of my family members at a rapid pace. If I'm mindless, this rush of negativity will lead me to pick fights. When I am well rested, these perceived flaws rarely come to mind. My awareness of this pattern allows me to recognize that a swarm of self-righteous criticisms swirling in my head reflects my fatigue, not inherent failings in my loved ones. Thus, when I observe crabby complaints proliferating in my mind, I try to recognize them for the friends they are, signaling me that it's time to get some rest.

Mindless "Right"-fulness

Have you seen that bumper sticker that says "Would you rather be right or happy?" Too often, especially during conflict, we put all of our energy into being right, at the expense of being happy.

Often disagreements occur because two people *feel different* about a topic. One person feels and thinks one way (*dirty dishes should never be left on the counter!),* and the other person has a different view *(it's more efficient to clean everything up at once later).* There's not a "right" way of doing things, but it sure feels like it in the moment, especially if the issue at hand is something you feel strongly about.

A fight like this is really about a difference in priorities or perspectives. If you are not careful, you can get stuck uselessly trying to convince your fellow combatant to feel or think the same way you feel or think. In these instances it may be more helpful to acknowledge your different views and put your energy into deciding whose perspective is going to be honored in the moment. First, you have to be willing to let go of the idea that the other person is flawed because he thinks differently than you do; then you can problem solve and work out a compromise. Is there some middle path that would allow you both to get what you want? Can you take turns getting what you want, prioritizing each person's most cared-about issue? You don't have to agree; you just have to be respectful of each other's feelings and opinions.

TAKE A MOMENT: Sometimes we need to speak hard truths, but sometimes we blurt out hurtful words, unhelpfully acting out our anger, jealousy, or resentment. Sometimes we are just nervously filling space with idle prattle. If we are not mindful, our careless words can unintentionally damage our most important relationships.

Buddhist meditation and Hindu Yogic traditions emphasize the importance of "right speech," which is essentially being thoughtful about what we say, doing our best to not cause unnecessary harm with our words. Words, unlike your pet dog, cannot be brought back once they escape, so it's important to think carefully before you let them loose. To work on right speech, try the following:

Before you speak, take a moment and ask yourself whether what you are about to say is *truthful* (you may be surprised how often you say things that are not exactly true), *necessary* (does it really need to be said?), *kind* (even disagreement can be expressed kindly), and *at the right moment* (an exhausted friend may not be in the best place to hear feedback). If what you have to say doesn't meet these criteria, maybe you should wait a bit and adjust your message, or just take some breaths and let the urge to speak pass entirely.

CONTEMPLATE THIS:

Our speech is powerful. It can be destructive and enlightening, idle gossip or compassionate communication. When we speak what is true and helpful, people are attracted to us. To be mindful and honest makes our minds quieter and more open, our hearts happier and more peaceful.

—Jack Kornfield

Listen More; Talk Less

Sometimes when I'm supposed to be listening to my partner, I'm really just preparing my rebuttal to whatever point he is making, thinking about why I am right and he is wrong. This jockeying to get the next word in blocks me from truly taking in whatever he is trying to say, and it thus blocks true communication. I'm pretty sure I'm not the only one who does this.

There is a mindfulness practice known as deep listening that helps improve communication. George Mumford (2015) describes deep listening as "the practice of stopping and listening without judgment or advice" (124). When you listen deeply, you tune in to what is being said, and tune out, as best you can, all the assumptions and arguments that bubble out of your brain. If you listen deeply, you are much more likely to actually hear and understand what is being said, a critical part of effective communication.

Practice Tip: Like all mindfulness skills, you can cultivate the ability to listen deeply by practicing it. During your next meditation session, open your observing mind to the sounds around you. Notice sounds near and far. Try not to hang on to them or push them away. See if you can hear them without naming or analyzing them. When thoughts and reactions are triggered, notice them with curiosity, then turn your attention back to what sounds your ears can detect.

Later, see if you can bring a similar level of nonjudgmental awareness to your next conversation. Be curious about your experience when you actively let go of the thoughts clamoring for expression and instead open yourself to fully hearing what is being communicated.

Respond More; React Less

One of the great benefits of mindfulness is that it allows you to respond thoughtfully, rather than react impulsively when something happens that triggers a quick burst of intense emotion.

Having the capacity to regulate your responses helps curb things like road rage and emotional overeating, but it is particularly valuable for navigating rocky moments in your relationships.

We have all experienced that wave of emotion that hits us when someone says something that pushes our most sensitive buttons; in an instant we blurt out a caustic comment that makes the situation worse and that we later regret.

Mindfulness helps by opening a tiny space between the onset of a wave of emotion and the eruption of words from your mouth. Your observing mind can slip into that space, feel the emotion in your body, see the impulse to react, and open awareness to other options. Taking a couple mindful breaths before you do anything else gives you a chance to respond more thoughtfully—or perhaps not at all. Staying aware in moments of emotional intensity can transform your relationships with family, friends, lovers, and bosses.

Mona described her experience with this. By taking a few breaths before responding, she headed off a fight with her girlfriend, Jasmine, who was angry because Mona had invited her sister to stay with them without first clearing it with Jasmine. Mona said, "Rather than do what I usually do, which is get super defensive and start criticizing her, I took a breath and waited for a bit. As I calmed down, I realized she kind of had a good point, so I told her that. We then had this calm conversation about how we both felt. It was so much better than our usual shouting matches."

Compliment More; Criticize Less

Here's a useful tip: You will be happier and your relationships will thrive if you keep the ratio of compliments to criticisms at 5:1. That means you need to make sure you make five kind, grateful, or agreeable comments for every single complaint or criticism you utter. That's right: five good things for every snarky thing. Doesn't matter if you have 100 complaints as long as you balance that with 500 compliments. (See Science Note below.)

Use this formula with all of your relationships: bosses, employees, teachers, roommates, lovers, mothers, brothers, friends. Everyone. If you are able to do this, your relationships will be healthier and you will be happier.

Intentionally finding the good in the people around you is a potent mindfulness exercise. Because of our mind's powerful negativity bias—the tendency to see bad things much more easily than good ones—it's much easier to notice the things we don't like in other people than the things we like. You have to be fully on your mindfulness game to balance this bias and pick up on all those interactions that are delightful, funny, and kind.

Once you start noticing the good, the next step is to actually share the love, which can be surprisingly hard. Ed laughed as he shared his experience trying to find something nice to say to his hypercritical roommate:

"Since we talked about how giving compliments can improve relationships, I've been trying to give my roommate at least one compliment a day. It's been hard because he's always complaining and he drives me crazy.

"First I could hardly think of anything—I mean, this guy is super annoying. Finally I was like, *Well, he does have good personal hygiene, and that's a really good thing in a roommate.* But that was just too weird a thing to say. Then I thought *I could give him some credit for being so quiet in the mornings and letting me sleep.* It was so hard to say anything nice to him, it felt like, I don't know, giving in to him or something. Finally though, I was like, 'Hey dude, I really appreciate that you're so quiet in the mornings. That's really nice. My old roommate used to wake me up all the time.' He looked at me sort of weird and I felt pretty much like an idiot.

"The next day he gave me a message from a friend who had stopped by, and I told him how much I appreciated him doing that. It seemed to get easier each day, and I swear, I'm not feeling so annoyed with him anymore.

And he seems more chill too, like maybe me saying nice things to him made him nicer to me. So things are better and that's cool."

Learning to see the good in others and say it aloud is a great skill that can smooth all your connections. It's especially valuable in your most intimate relationships. You may assume that your partner knows how smart or attractive or funny you think she is, but if you don't say it clearly to her, she may feel that she only hears from you when you have a complaint or nag. Remember, she has a negativity bias as well, which is why she will need to hear five expressions of adoration to make up for each grouse or grumble.

Unless we balance our complaints with extra compliments, over time resentments build up that erode the foundations of our relationships. When we speak our appreciations aloud, it helps remind us what we value in our friends, lovers, and family members and helps them feel valued as well.

Science Note: John Gottman has studied married couples for many years in his lab at the University of Washington in Seattle. By watching couples disagree and tracking the way they go about resolving conflict, he has developed models for predicting which relationships will have staying power. In the lab, he videotapes couples while they discuss problem areas in their relationships. He and his colleagues then tally the negative comments (things like complaints, defensiveness, and criticisms) and positive comments (things like humor or agreement). Gottman discovered that the overall amount of conflict was irrelevant. A stable and happy relationship could have any amount of conflict as long as the ratio of positive to negative interactions was at least 5:1 (Gottman 1994).

TAKE A MOMENT: Develop the habit of sharing compliments, and get started on it right now. Give the next person you see an authentic compliment. Notice something you admire or appreciate about him and tell him. Do this three times every day for the next week; it could be the same person or a different person each time. Have fun with it and be creative. Stay curious about what happens to your feelings toward the recipients of your compliments.

Bringing mindfulness to your relationships helps you build authentic, supportive connections—the kind of connections we all need to carry us through the rough patches and to share our pleasure when the living is good.

Using your meditation practice to identify your feelings without immediately reacting to them will enhance all your interactions. Take a few minutes now to practice the labeling feelings meditation in (see section entitled "Labeling Your Feelings").

As we near the end of this book, it's now time to reflect on your mindfulness practice and consider where you might want to take it next.

Chapter 19

Is Mindfulness for You?

The time has finally come for you to assess your experience with mindfulness. In the introduction, I invited you to experiment with mindfulness while you made your way through this book, waiting until the end before forming any opinions about its usefulness for you. Since you've hung in there with me, learning the mindfulness skills and meditations contained in these pages, you probably now have some data points you can analyze. So let's reflect.

What Have You Found?

Since you started this exploration, what changes, if any, have you noticed in your life? Are there subtle shifts in the way you handle stress? Do you notice yourself reacting with more equanimity to situations that would have distressed you before? Are you a bit more patient with yourself and others? Have you had any insights into the way your mind works that intrigued you? Are you noticing seeds of happiness starting to sprout? Have there been any shifts in your relationships? Answer these questions for yourself as honestly as you can.

If you have an inkling that these benefits are starting to accrue, then by all means keep building your mindfulness muscle. If you haven't noticed any changes, you may be wondering what all the fuss is about. I'm not sure why it is that mindfulness hooks some people and not others. Some say you have to amass a surplus of suffering before you see the appeal of the path that leads away from it. Maybe there is some truth in that. Personally, I got hooked pretty quickly because I almost immediately noticed benefits like worrying less about my future and enjoying my life more—enough so that I was motivated to persist, even when it wasn't easy. If, like me, you are galvanized to keep exploring, I've got some ideas about what you could do next.

What Next?

I doubt many of you, my readers, will decide to move into caves in the mountains and dedicate your lives for years to the cultivation of your minds, ultimately achieving full enlightenment. It's worth noting, though, that it is usually young adults who have the freedom and curiosity to travel abroad and work for years with a guru to plumb the depths of their minds. Still, it seems more likely you'll want to more gradually expand your practice, so let's consider how you can do that.

1. **Take a class or join a group.** Our culture is an anti-mindfulness culture, emphasizing doing over being, multitasking over giving full attention to one moment at a time. Connecting with others who have a similar interest in mindfulness will make your journey much easier.

    My first meditation teacher, Jeff Brantley, told me that if I really wanted to learn mindfulness, I would need a meditation group to sit with. He directed me to a group that I sat with every Wednesday night for almost twenty years. That group is the only reason that my practice advanced the way it did. There is no way I would have stuck with it without that community of fellow meditators.

    If you have just finished a Koru Basic class, you can sign up for the next Koru class, Koru 2.0. If you don't have a Koru teacher near you, not to worry—there is probably some other type of mindfulness group or class nearby. Ask the oracle, Ms. Google, what is out there, then muster up your courage and give it a try. Almost everybody feels a bit nervous or uncomfortable the first time they visit a new group; be mindful of your unease and go anyway. Visit three times before you form an opinion. The first time I visited the meditation group I ultimately joined, I felt awkward and restless, and I doubted it would ever feel like a comfortable space for me. If I'd made a final judgment about my group after that first visit, I never would have gone back. By the third time, I had a better sense of how it could be helpful to me.

If you can't find a class or group near you, then make your own group by convincing a few friends to join you. Plan to meet weekly for an hour or more. Use the time to meditate together and learn more about mindfulness. A useful format is a twenty-to thirty-minute meditation period followed by twenty to thirty minutes of reading together or listening to a podcast on mindfulness and then discussing it. Having friends hold you to the intention of a weekly meditation is a great way to support your practice.

2. **Attend a retreat.** Doing an extended meditation in the context of an organized retreat is the best way, bar none, to see the potential of mindfulness in your life.

    Mindfulness meditation retreats are typically held in silence with alternating periods of sitting meditation and walking meditation. The meditations are typically broken up only by delicious, mindful meals and inspiring talks by the teachers. Retreats can be as short as half a day or as long as several months. Typical lengths are three to seven days.

I know that the idea of silently meditating for several days sounds scary. I remember when I first heard about retreats from friends who had attended them; I told them that sounded awful and that I would never try a retreat. But as my mother used to assert, the less you say, the less you have to take back. My strongly expressed aversion to retreats turned out to be just one more thing I've had to take back.

Over the years I've done many retreats, some more challenging for me than others. My first three-day retreat was very hard; I was restless and struggled the entire time. My first seven-day retreat was the most amazing, mind-blowing experience I'd ever had. I remember chatting with another participant at the end of the retreat who told me that he'd never meditated for even a minute in his life before the start of the retreat. He'd chosen the retreat over the opportunity to raft the Grand Canyon. He concluded that he had made the right choice, saying that the consciousness-changing experience of the retreat was a wilder adventure than any rafting trip could have been.

There are many retreat centers across the country and many great teachers leading retreats. To find one near you, search the web for "mindfulness meditation," "insight meditation," or "Vipassana" retreats.

3. **Keep learning.** Find a teacher, read books, listen to podcasts, visit websites, and go to talks about mindfulness and meditation. The more you explore the topic, the more you will feel inspired to keep practicing. The more you practice, the more you will benefit, which will in turn lead to more exploration and growth.

I hope you decide to take these suggestions and run with them, building your mindfulness practice so that you live the many but finite days of your life with greater awareness. Whether you simply manage your stress with a few minutes of mindful breathing a day or invest many hours exploring the depths of your consciousness, mindfulness offers you the possibility of living with greater ease and deeper meaning. It might be nice to fully embrace the absolute wonder of your life before too much more of it has passed.

Chapter 20

For the Benefit of All

I end each of my personal meditation sessions by holding my hands in front of my heart in a prayer position and saying silently to myself, *May my practice be for the benefit of all beings.* I think I learned this at a retreat led by Joseph Goldstein that I attended many years ago. Doing this gives me a sense of my connection to others and the world. This feeling of connection has grown along with my meditation practice and the recognition that everybody everywhere wants the same thing: to suffer less.

I am far from perfect, but I know that my meditation practice makes me travel through this life with a bit more ease and a bit more to offer others. I believe my practice has made me a smidgen kinder and wiser. I think I am better able to see humor in the silliness of life, celebrate differences, and forgive foibles. Though it may be just wishful thinking, it seems to me that these little changes in myself make tiny ripples that flow into the world, making someone else's life a little easier, who in turn then makes someone else's life a little easier, and so on. And of course, I benefit from these little ripples too, as many of them wash back toward me.

When my daughter was young, we used to read a picture book about a hen who gave an egg to her friend the pig, who was feeling sad. The pig was so grateful for the hen's generosity that he paid the gift forward to another friend in need, and so on. At the end of the story, the egg made it all the way back around to the original giver, the hen, who then benefitted from the chain of generosity and kindness she had started when the egg hatched into an adorable little chick. Maybe our acts of thoughtfulness and generosity can create chains of positive change, like a little gift passed endlessly from one person to the next.

As a young adult, you likely have many years ahead of you to watch the results of positive change compound and grow over time. Even small shifts in your life course in your twenties can produce profound benefits over the full arc of your life, both for you and for those with whom your life path intersects.

The idea that small changes produce big impacts is a hopeful one. I love watching YouTube videos of Rube Goldberg machines, seeing how a small domino falling can set in motion a complex series of events that ultimately produces a simple desired outcome like the opening of a door. Perhaps like a giant Rube Goldberg machine, our positive words and deeds create a domino effect, triggering a chain of events that surrounds the planet, ultimately opening wide a window on a better world for all.

Thank you for joining me on this journey. May your practice take you to places that surprise you and elevate you. May your practice be for the benefit of all.

Acknowledgments

This book is largely a result of my good fortune in having been guided, helped, and supported by so many wise and compassionate others. With no hope of doing justice to all who have helped me, or recognizing all to whom I am indebted, I want to offer my acknowledgment and thanks to the following people:

I am eternally grateful to Jeff Brantley, my teacher and mentor who started me on this path and remains a source of support and wisdom for my endeavors. I'd like to thank all my colleagues at Duke University's Counseling and Psychological Services, including the directors past and present who have supported the development of Koru and given me the time and space I have needed to develop and grow the program. Koru would not exist but for the wisdom and warmth of the wonderful Margaret Maytan, to whom I send a deep bow of gratitude.

A number of patient people have read and/or given me advice about this book, including Sophia Nasrullah, Will Price, Leigh Egeghy, Ayesha Chaudhary, Stacie McEntyre, Ann Gleason, Katelyn Ander, and Richard Jaffe. I owe a particular debt to my dear friends and wise advisors, Libby Webb and Jennie Dickson,

210

who have taken on the tedious task of reading and advising me on every word in my manuscript.

The folks at New Harbinger have been a delight to work with. Particular thanks go to Wendy Millstine, Vicraj Gill, and Tesilya Hanauer, my very patient editor. I offer a special thanks to Rona Bernstein for putting the final polish on the project.

This book most certainly would not have made it to press without the patient and loving support of my husband, Bill Price, and my daughter, Maggie Rose Price.

Finally, I am perhaps most indebted to the hundreds of students who have participated in Koru at Duke. Truly none of this would have happened without their great energy, curiosity, and enthusiasm. Thank you, all.

References

Arnett, J. 2004. *Emerging Adulthood: The Winding Road from the Late Teens Through the Twenties.* New York: Oxford University Press.

Brown, K.W. 2013. *Adulting: How to Become a Grown-Up in 468 Easy(ish) Steps.* New York: Grand Central Publishing.

Byrd, R. (1938) 2003. *Alone: The Classic Polar Adventure.* Reprint, Washington, DC: Island Press. Originally published by G.P. Putnam's Sons.

Carlson, R. 1996. *Don't Sweat the Small Stuff ... And It's All Small Stuff.* New York: Hachette Books.

Condon, P., G. Desbordes, W. Miller, and D. DeSteno. 2013. "Meditation Increases Compassionate Responses to Suffering." *Psychological Science,* 24 (10): 2125–27.

"Effects of Sexual Activity on Beard Growth in Man." 1970. *Nature* 226: 869–870.

Emmons, R. 2007. *Thanks!* New York: Houghton Mifflin.

Fox, K., S. Nijeboer, M. Dixon, J. Floman, M. Ellamil, S. Rumak, P. Sedlmeier, and K. Christoff. 2014. "Is Meditation Associated with Altered Brain Structure? A Systematic Review and Meta-analysis of Morphometric Neuroimaging in Meditation Practitioners." *Neuroscience and Behavioral Reviews* 43: 48–73.

Fronsdal, G. 2008. *The Issue at Hand.* Ontario: Bookland.

Gottman, J.M. 1994. *What Predicts Divorce? The Relationship Between Marital Processes and Marital Outcomes.* Hillsdale, NJ: Lawrence Erlbaum Associates.

Greeson, J., M. Juberg, M. Maytan, K. James, and H. Rogers. 2014. "A Randomized, Controlled Trial of Koru: A Mindfulness Program for College Students and Other Emerging Adults." *Journal of American College Health* 62 (4): 222–33.

Gunaratana, H. 2001. *Eight Mindful Steps to Happiness.* Boston: Wisdom Publications.

_____. 1996. *Mindfulness in Plain English.* Boston: Wisdom.

Haidt, J. 2006. *The Happiness Hypothesis.* New York: Basic Books.

Harris, D. 2014. *10% Happier.* New York: Harper Collins Publishers.

Iyer, P. 2014. *The Art of Stillness.* New York: Simon and Schuster, Inc.

Kabat-Zinn, J. (1990) 2013. *Full Catastrophe Living.* New York: Bantam Books.

_____. 2005. *Wherever You Go, There You Are.* New York: Hachette Books.

Kraft, T., and S. Pressman. 2012. "Grin and Bear It: The Influence of Manipulated Facial Expression on the Stress Response." *Psychological Science* 23 (11): 1372–78.

Lyubomirsky, S., K. Sheldon, and D. Schkade. 2005. "Pursuing Happiness: The Architecture of Sustainable Change." *Review of General Psychology* 9 (2): 111–31.

Mumford, G. 2015. *The Mindful Athlete: Secrets to Pure Performance.* Berkeley, CA: Parallax Press.

Northeastern University. 2015. *Can Meditation Make You a More Compassionate Person?* Accessed October 25, 2015. http://www.north eastern.edu/cos/2013/04/release-can-meditatio n-make-you-a-more-compassionate-person/.

Nyhan, B., and J. Reifler. 2010. "When Corrections Fail: The Persistence of Political Misperceptions." *Political Behavior* 32: 303–30.

Ricard, M. 2006. *Happiness: A Guide to Developing Life's Most Important Skill.* New York: Little, Brown and Company.

Seery, M., E. Homan, and R. Silver. 2010. "Whatever Does Not Kill Us: Cumulative Lifetime Adveristy, Vulnerability, and Resilience." *Journal of Personality and Social Psychology* 99 (6): 1025–41.

Simmons, R. 2014. *Success Through Stillness.* New York: Gotham Books.

Suzuki, S. 1970. *Zen Mind, Beginner's Mind.* Edited by Trudy Dixon. Boulder, CO: John Weatherhill, Inc.

Tolle, E. 2004. *The Power of Now.* Vancouver, British Columbia: Namaste Publishing.

Weger, U., N. Hooper, B. Meier, and T. Hopthrow. 2012. "Mindful Maths: Reducing the Impact of Stereotype Threat Through a Mindfulness Exercise." *Consciousness and Cognition* 21: 471–75.

Holly B. Rogers, MD, is a psychiatrist and mindfulness teacher at Duke University's student counseling center. Along with Margaret Maytan, MD, she developed Koru Mindfulness, the only evidence-based mindfulness training program designed specifically for college-age adults. Coauthor of *Mindfulness for the Next Generation,* Rogers is one of the leading experts on teaching mindfulness to young adults.

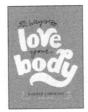

Back Cover Material

THIS IS YOUR LIFE. DON'T MISS IT.

Your twenties are about finding out who you really are. But between work, relationships, and planning for the future, you may feel like you're being pulled in a dozen different directions. The key to making the most of these transformative years is learning to be fully present in the moment, in good times and bad. So, how can you stay grounded when life is rushing by?

This mindful guide offers a unique approach for navigating your twenties with clarity and confidence. You'll learn to tackle stress, gain a healthier perspective, get in touch with what really matters to you, and make important life decisions guided by self-knowledge and understanding. Most importantly, you'll discover mindfulness techniques to manage life's day-today challenges from a calm, balanced center—a useful skill at any age.

"A 21st CENTURY BOOK, GROUNDED IN ANCIENT WAYS OF PRACTICE."
—SHARON SALZBERG, author of *Lovingkindness* and *Real Happiness*

"THIS BOOK IS AN EXCELLENT RESOURCE FOR A PERSON OF 'ANY-SOMETHING' AGE

WHO WISHES TO BEGIN OR LEARN MORE ABOUT PRACTICING MINDFULNESS."
—JEFF BRANTLEY, MD, author of *Calming Your Angry Mind*

"WISE, BUT NOT OBSCURE. PRACTICAL, BUT LIGHTHEARTED AND INSPIRING."
—MIRABAI BUSH, meditation and mindfulness teacher

HOLLY B. ROGERS, MD, is a psychiatrist and mindfulness teacher at Duke University's student counseling center. Along with Margaret Maytan, MD, she developed Koru Mindfulness, a popular mindfulness training program for college-aged adults. Rogers is coauthor of *Mindfulness for the Next Generation.*

CPSIA information can be obtained
at www.ICGtesting.com
Printed in the USA
BVHW011521190820
R11098800001B/R110988PG585870BVX1B/1